Tribal Bible

Stories of God from Oral Tradition

Runyon, Daniel V.
Tribal Bible: Stories of God from Oral Tradition
ISBN: 978-1-878559-15-9

Cover design by Kwade Joslin

Copyright 2014 by Daniel V. Runyon
All rights reserved.

For information contact:
    Daniel V. Runyon
    167 Burr Oak Drive
    Spring Arbor, MI 49283
    dvrunyon@gmail.com

Printed in the United States of America
Price: $20.00

Preface

To restore the twelve sons of Jacob to their rightful place is a very easy thing for me; I will also make you a light for all people—you will bring my salvation to the ends of the earth. —Isaiah 49:6

Into their minds will I put my law; on their hearts will I write it.... Everyone in all tribes will know me from the most important chiefs to the least of the women and children. —Jeremiah 31:33-34

This is our agreement: "The Lord said, 'My spirit which is on you, and my words which are in you, will always be on your mouth and on the mouths of your children and their children—from now on—for all time.'" —Isaiah 59:21

Good news of the rule of God will be taught to every family living on planet Earth, and then will come the end. —Matthew 24:14

I saw another angel flying in mid-heaven. He had the eternal good news to preach over the ones sitting on the earth: over every nation and tribe and tongue and people. —Revelation 14:6

Contents

page	Section
6	**Introduction**
7	**1. In the Beginning**
	A story from the grandfather of McPherson Janaia Banda: *A Clay Baby*
23	**2. Seeds of Abraham**
	A story from the grandfather of Blessings Chagomerana: *Akafula for Short*
46	**3. Migration and Return**
	A story from the grandmother of Hawa Phiri: *Snake! Snake! Snake!*
71	**4. Expatriates Restored**
	A story from the grandfather of Fred Bamus: *The Widow Mary Lynod*
93	**5. A. Expected One —Predictions Come True**
	A story from the village of Chifundo Patrick: *Ready to Be Rich*
116	**B. Expected One—Saving the People**
	A story from the grandfather of George Lupande: *The Nomad Chief*

131	**C. Expected One—Suffering Servant** A story from the mother of MacDonald Chikankheni: *A One-Eyed Mum*
154 **6.**	**God's People Today** A story from the grandfather of Ronald Chinkonde: *Matola Tola*
175 **7.**	**In the New Beginning** A story from the father of George Chikoya: *The HIV Hyena*
196	**Tribal Bible Origins**
205	**Acknowledgements**
206	**Dedication**

Introduction

Please read this book as you would a novel—just start at the beginning and read straight through. Each section begins with a tribal legend containing nuggets of truth followed by true stories of God as told by Africans in the style of their oral traditions. Taken together, these short stories narrate the history of the world from the first creation to the new creation, and phrased in ways understood by village people.

The name of each tribal author appears at the beginning of each story along with the Bible reference on which the story is based. These stories were first told in various languages of Malawi, Africa, and then translated into English. The story sequence narrates a fascinating plot that reveals the purposes of God in human history.

—*Daniel V. Runyon*, Editor

Section 1: In the Beginning

The word "Genesis" comes from the Greek translation of the Hebrew word *toledot* or "story" (Gen. 2:4). From the beginning, God has chosen to reveal himself through stories. When we tell stories of our own, we exhibit one of the many ways we are made in his image.

McPherson Janaia Banda says stories are told in his African village because his people do not want to forget the culture and reputations of their forefathers. Story telling is also a matter of passing the hours away, of entertaining the children, and of counseling and giving some warnings. Here is a favorite story of his, learned from his grandfather:

A Clay Baby

There was a family that had no baby, so one day the man thought, "If I can make bricks from the mud, maybe I can make a baby the same way." So he molded mud into the image of a baby, breathed air into the drying image, and it started to breathe. The man gave careful instructions to this clay baby, that to avoid melting away, it must never touch the water or drink the water.

One day the clay baby went to the garden to do a certain piece of work without noticing the weather. It was the rainy season and suddenly the sky began to change. Clouds gathered. Lightning began to flash. Thunder shook the garden. The clay baby understood this danger and hurried toward home. This would take some time since it was a distant journey.

Rain soon fell heavily. Soon the clay baby became completely wet and started melting. When he was about a meter from his dwelling, he completely dissolved away. His parents felt very sorry and cried bitterly over the loss of their beloved clay baby.

The story teaches us that, no matter how important we might be, we need to obey our parents to avoid problems.

Stories from Genesis 1-11

In the beginning God made the sky and earth. A wind from God swept over the watery darkness. "Let there be light," God spoke, and there was light. He made light and darkness separate things, and that concluded his first task of bringing order out of chaos.

Then God separated water into two kinds: liquid water that runs on the ground and vapor water that stays in the air. God made an expanse that he called sky, and that concluded his second task.

God then shifted the earth in a way that put water in some areas and allowed dry land to appear in other places. He called the water sea and the land Earth. "Let the earth sprout every kind of plant from seeds," God said, and the earth grew every kind of vegetation, each plant bearing seeds to produce more of that same plant. And God saw that this was a good result of his third task.

God's fourth invention was to make the sun to light and heat the earth and to separate day and night, and the moon and stars to light the night. He placed them in the sky to shine upon the earth and saw that this was good.

"Let the waters swarm with living creatures," God said next, and sea monsters and living creatures of every kind that creep about and swarm in the waters grew and reproduced. He also filled the sky with winged birds of every kind that fly, and he blessed them and said for them to fill the earth. That concluded his fifth big task.

Then God did the same thing on the land, filling the earth with all the walking creatures: cattle, creeping things, and wild beasts. God saw that this was good, and then he said, "Let us make mankind in our image, after our likeness. They shall rule all the living things: the sea creatures, the sky creatures, and the earth creatures."

That was God's ultimate creative work: He made mankind in the image of God; male and female. He blessed them and said, "Be fertile and increase, fill the earth and master it. See, I give you every seed-bearing plant and fruit-bearing tree for food, just as I give green plants for food to every creature that has the breath of life in it." And it was so. God looked at everything he had made and found it to be very good, and that brought to an end the sixth creative task of his.

So heaven and earth were finished! On the seventh day God stopped all the work of creation and rested. He blessed the seventh day and called it holy. Such is the story of the things of God as he was making the heaven and earth.

P. Alufasi Phiri (Gen. 2)

The Account of the Heaven and the Earth

When God created the heavens and the earth he also made a man out of the dust of the ground and breathed into his nose the breath of life. The Lord planted a garden for him to rule over in Eden, and he watered the garden with four rivers. All the animals and living things were both female and male, but Adam had no suitable helper. Then the Lord caused Adam to sleep and from his side made a woman and brought her to the man. Adam received her and gave thanks to the Lord and lived with her. At that time both were naked and they felt no shame.

George Lupande (Gen. 2)

The Great Designer

How great are your hands, O Lord.

You are the great designer.

The earth is the work of your hands.

Even the dry land produces shrubs that cover us,

    avoiding the warmth from the sun.

The streams of water flow according to your plans.

The wonders shall never end.

From your mouth comes a living thing.

These great and beautiful trees

    are also the work of your hands,

And from the dust comes a man.

From your mouth the man starts his first breath.

The man looked here and there; he was alone.

Because of your mercy and love,

    you made a companion for him

A very suitable helper.
From his ribs the beautiful gift came.
The man's eyes opened widely,
    amazed with the lovely one.
How beautiful was she—like lemons
    along the Euphrates River.
The flesh of the man, now woman
    —her name is Eve.
You gave them authority to rule.
All the earth is under their care.

P. Alufasi Phiri (Gen. 2:4-25)

Song of Creation

Praise be to you, O Lord, God Almighty,
For the wonderful creation you have made!
Glory be to you from the heavens and the earth
For out of nothing you made our earth and heavens.
O God Almighty you have done everything in order.
Praise be to you for the rains;
    praise for the streams, praise for the rivers.
Plants and animals also praise you
    for your wonderful love.
Both get their need from you
    through sun and water and rest.

God Almighty, praise to you
> for making man from dust.

From the dust of the ground you have made a man!
You are the breath of life. You breathed into the man
And the man became a living being. Praise to you!
You put the man in a right place,
> you gave him the garden of Eden.

You are worthy to be honored,
> for you gave him all things to eat.

From his side you took a woman!
Now man is never alone.
The two become one; they manifest your love.
There is no shame among the man and woman,
> there is only love.

For you are the One who first shows love.
Praise and glory be upon you
> for the beautiful and orderly world. Amen.

George M. Chikoya (Gen. 3:1-24)

Oh! The Serpent!

Oh! The serpent! What a great deceiver are you.
You have deceived my mamie and dadie
> in the garden of Eden.

Oh! The serpent!

You're more crafty than any wild animals today.

My mamie, Eve, Why have you heard this deceiver?

Why are you respecting him as your husband Adam?

Oh! The serpent!

Why are you talking to Eve as your wife?

How wiser are you than God?

Don't touch, don't eat, the fruit from the middle tree.

Don't you hear the caution from God?

Oh! Eve!

Why don't you say "no" to the serpent?

"Yes" to evil brings death. Don't you know that?

Oh! The serpent!

Let me tell you this: you will crawl on your belly;

Enmity will be between a man and you.

Your head will be crushed.

Oh! My mamie Eve!

I have millions of questions for you,

But for today just answer me three:

Are you like God as the serpent told you?

Why have you been found naked in the garden?

Why are you hiding; why feeling pains giving birth?

Oh! My mamie! God feels pity with you.

My dadie Adam,

Where are you now? Don't you hear from God?

The ground is cursed because you listened to Eve!

Why thorns? Why thistles? Why are you sweating?
Why? Why death now and again, here and there?
Oh! The serpent!
A great deceiver indeed.

McPherson Banda (Gen. 4)
The Song of Adam and Eve for Abel

O, the Lord our God, bring us peace and harmony. We have seen how evil Satan is. We have noticed how the devil deceives people. O God, deliver us from such deceitful ways.

You blessed us by a beloved son named Abel who has been slashed down by evil in spite of your acceptance of his offering. Jealous and angry, his brother deceived Abel by calling him to the field where he might fulfill his evil desire, and there he struck him down to die. We praise you the Lord because everything is always done in the presence of your sight. You helped us by chasing the killer from the land, and you cursed that land of his. Yet you are a God of love and listened even to the request of that one! You placed a mark on his face as a sign of forgiveness and he settled in the land of Nod. O Lord, we thank you because you blessed us with another son, Seth, in replace of Abel.

L. L. B. Kachinjika (Gen.6-8)

Song of the Flood

Praise to the Lord Almighty
    who made the earth and all in it.
Who said to his people and his creatures,
    be fruitful, increase in number.

Woe to the generation of Noah who departed from God.
Their minds became evil and their eyes were blinded.
But God saw their evil and shortened their years of living.

Foolish is the man who made God to fill with pain.
Soon God will wipe you away
And destroy your nation completely.

Blessed is the one who finds favor in God's eyes,
Who is righteous and blameless?
He is able to walk with God.

God reveals secrets to the man who walks with him;
He will escape the wrath of God.
He will be assigned work

and will receive instructions for making things.

Who can make covenant with God?
Noah is the one who keeps his instructions.
Who is obedient to God's word?
Who has great love to save all creatures
From being destroyed?
Only God does this.

The righteous man will enter the ark of God.
The wicked will be wiped away.
The ark of God is a refuge for those who fear the Lord.

Who can gather together all the creatures of the earth?
Only Noah, with power from the almighty God.
They saved male and female animals and birds
    in the days of God's righteous servant Noah.

Honor to God Almighty who opens the springs of water.
He opens heaven's floodgates and sends down rain.
His name is Yahweh who floods the earth
    in the days of his blameless servant Noah.
He destroys all who do evil in his sight.

Who can stand against the judgment of God?

Even the highest mountains cannot stand against him.
He covers them with the waters—glory to his name!
If he opens, no one can close; if he closes, no one can open.

He is the God almighty
> who commanded the floodgates and rains to stop.

He made the floods of waters to dry up
> in the days of his true servant Noah.

Who can stand before God?
Who can sacrifice burnt offerings that please the Lord?
Noah can!
With the sweet smell of aromatic sacrifices
> he worships God.

The God of Noah has great love for his creation.
He swears that he will never again destroy living creatures
> because of the evil of men.

Your name is Jehovah.
Glory to you for ever and ever,
Amen.

MacDonald Chikankheni (Gen. 9)

A Big Hand for Noah

He could not even think or even understand, having looked afar and seen no man moving nor the sound of any creature that he was used to hear before the flood, except that of his family and creatures that came out from the boat with him.

Still waiting for heavenly directions, Noah finally heard the word of blessing from the Lord: "Be fruitful, increase in number, and fill the earth and even have dominion over all creation. Do you see those beautiful trees and their fruits, and even these fat animals, Noah? They are there for your food. But only be warned of this: do not eat meat with its life blood in it, or even from your own blood I will demand an accounting. To maintain peace among you, no man should shed another man's blood.

"Maybe, Noah, you live afraid about any harm from me. So now I give you my own words marking the establishment of my covenant with you, your sons, your descendants, and even the creatures that came out with you from the ark: Never will flood waters destroy the earth again. I will set a rainbow in the clouds that will always remind me of this everlasting covenant whenever I bring clouds over the earth."

Now my friend, do you know how God saved you and me in this time? It is through three sons of this righteous man by their names of Ham, Shem, and Japheth. Noah enjoyed the life again, but because it is for a man to die, Noah died after living for 950 years.

A big hand for Noah!

Nelson Banda (Gen. 11)

The Tower of Babel

Once there was one language in the world and these Babylonians thought to use bricks to build a tower at Shinar. The Lord Almighty came down to see the tower and he was not pleased. Instead he brought new languages so they would not understand each other, and they started to move around the world. Babel, now see what you have done! People speak different languages because of you! You babble when you speak against the Lord.

William Billiat (Gen. 11)

The Song of Babel

I feel sorry in my heart when I see people in Babel—
    the fall of Babylon
Having desire to emphasize themselves like God—

    the fall of Babylon.

Chorus:

The fall of Babylon

    makes a great changing in the world.

The fall of Babylon

    makes a great changing in the world

    For misinterpretation of the Word of God.

The arrogant people make bricks and mortar—

    yet Babylon will fall.

They build a city that reaches heaven—

    yet Babylon will fall.

They fail because our God is wonderful—

    and Babylon will fall.

These people had one language—

    before the fall of Babylon.

They worried God by common speech—

    before the fall of Babylon.

God confused them by giving different languages—

    before the fall of Babylon

He scattered them like bees to south and north—

    at the fall of Babylon.

Don't be like the people of Babel,

>but give praise and thanks to God.
God knows our thinking before we do,
>give praise and thanks to God.
If we depend upon ourselves,
>we'll fall like Babylon.

Section 2: Seeds of Abraham

A story from the grandfather of Blessings Chagomerana:

Akafula for Short

A long time ago in Nyasaland a group of people called Akafula always fought against the Chewa and Ngoni. At the beginning the Chewa people came here from Zaire because of war. The Ngoni people also came here and they were all living together as one.

The Chewa were like kings because they were the first to come, but there were no problems with the Ngoni. They all lived together sharing things. Then more tribes came and the population increased. Then the Akafula came to Nyasaland, but instead of just living as friends, they started fighting.

The Akafuna were very short—no more than one and one-half meters tall—and they did not want to be under the leadership of the Chewa. They would always fight other people. For example, if an Akafula person was walking along the way and met someone not from his tribe, he would ask, "How far away did you see me?"

If you answered, "I did not see you until we came very close together," then the Akafula would fight you for insulting him for being so short. But if you said, "I saw you coming from far away," then you would have honored him for being tall and that might have kept him from fighting you.

So the Akafula kept fighting the Chewa until they were at last defeated. Some ran away back to Zaire, some went other places and scattered, and a few still live here. Now days if someone is very short, people will say they are Akafula as a way of mocking them.

Stories from Genesis 12-45

One day God told Abraham he must leave his country and his people and his father's house and go to a place which God would show him, a place called Canaan. God said he would make Abraham into a great nation and bless him, and curse those who curse him.

So Abraham did what God told him to do. In that time Abraham was already 75 years old, and he took his nephew Lot and his wife, Sarah, and he followed where God led. When he got there, the Lord appeared to him and said he would give him this land. So Abraham built an altar in that place to the Lord. And he pitched his tent in a place called Bethel.

Winiko Wanyetha (Gen. 13-14)

The First Communion

So Abraham went from place to place and by the time he came to Bethel he had become very rich. There he built an altar to acknowledge the Lord. His nephew Lot was also with him, but the land could not support their many flocks and herds, so quarreling arose between Abraham's men and Lot's men.

"Let there be no fighting between us," Abraham said, and invited Lot to choose where he would like to live. Lot noticed that the whole plain of the Jordan had water, like the garden of the Lord, so he chose that place to live and pitched his tents near Sodom. Now the men of Sodom were sinning against the Lord.

But Abraham lived in Canaan. One day the Lord said to him, "Lift up your eyes to look as far as you can see. I will give all this land to you and to your offspring forever. I will make your people as many as the dust of the earth. So Abraham obeyed God and did everything God said to do.

The day came when four kings seized all the goods of Sodom and Gomorrah and carried them away, even taking Abraham's nephew Lot and all his possessions. One who had escaped came and reported this news to Abraham.

Abraham was living near the great trees of Mamre, and when he heard the news, he took 318 of his trained men and overtook those four kings and defeated them. He recovered all the goods and brought back his relative Lot as well as all his possessions together with the women and the other people.

Then Melchizedek King of Salem brought out a sacred meal of bread and wine. He was priest of God most high, and he blessed Abraham saying, "Blessed be Abraham by God most high, Creator of the heaven and earth. And blessed be God most high who delivered your enemies into your hand." So Abraham gave to Melchizedek (who was a prophet, priest, and king all at the same time) a tenth of everything he had recovered from those four kings, and he praised the Lord.

P. Alufasi Phiri (Gen. 15, 17)

Covenant

The time came when God went to fulfill what he had planned already for Abraham. So God came and talked with Abraham in a vision while he and his wife were childless. He said to Abraham, "Don't be afraid. I am your shield and your very great reward."

But Abraham was doubting. "What can you give me?" he wondered. "My wife and I are very old, yet we remain childless. The one who will inherit my estate is Eliezer of Damascus, and he will be my heir."

God said that Eliezer is not the one, but the son coming out of your own body will be the one. God said his offspring would be like stars in the heavens. Therefore Abraham believed the Lord, a very righteous act.

God also said, "I am the Lord who brought you out of Ur of the Chaldeans to give you this land." So God commanded Abraham to bring a heifer, a goat, a ram, and other sacrifices, and he did so. Abraham obeyed everything God told him to do.

So one day when the sun was setting God came to talk with Abraham. He said, "Know for certain that your descendants will be strangers in a country not their own, and they will be enslaved and mistreated during four hundred years, but I will punish the nation they serve as slaves, and afterward they will come out with great possessions." And God promised Abraham the land from the river of Egypt to the great river.

Hawa Phiri (Gen. 16)

Hagar and Ishmael

Abraham's wife Sarah had borne him no children, but she had an Egyptian maidservant named Hagar, so she said to her husband, "Because the Lord has kept me from having children, go and sleep with my maidservant. Perhaps I can build a family through her, so I give you Hagar to be your wife." So Abraham slept with Hagar and she became pregnant.

When Hagar knew she was pregnant, she became proud and showed no respect to her mistress Sarah. This distressed Sarah and she complained to Abraham saying, "I am suffering now. I chose the wrong way when I put my servant to your arms. Now she despises me. May the Lord judge you and me."

"Whatever you think best is fine with me," he replied. "She is your servant."

So Hagar was sent away into the desert. The angel of the Lord found her near a spring of water, and he said to her, "Hagar servant of Sarah, where have you come from, and where are you going?"

"I am running away from my mistress," she replied. The angel of the Lord encouraged her to go back to her mistress and submit to her. And the angel said, "I will so increase your descendants that they will be too numerous to count. The angel also told her to name the son that she carried Ishmael, which means "the Lord has heard your misery."

The angel also told Hagar the son will be a wild donkey of a man. His hand will be against everyone, and everyone will be against him, and he will live in hostility toward all his brothers.

"You are the God who sees me," Hagar said, and she called the well in that place Beer-lahai-roi. So Hagar bore Abraham a son named Ishmael when Abraham was 86 years old.

Chifundo Patrick (Gen. 18-19)

Three visitors; Destruction of Sodom

Abraham was sitting at the entrance to his tent during a very hot day when he saw three men standing near a great tree of Mamre. He stood up to welcome them and said they should come to his tent and rest. While his wife Sarah prepared a meal, these guests discussed many things with Abraham. They asked about the town of Sodom, and they promised Abraham that he and his wife Sarah would have a son called Isaac even though they were already old and well advanced in years. Then the three guests said, "I will come again next year at this same time."

Before they left his tent, these men said they were going to destroy Sodom, so Abraham walked along with them because he knew that his nephew Lot was living in that wicked town. So he questioned them, asking if they would destroy the city if they found some people there who were righteous. The visitors said no, they would not destroy the city if they found 50 righteous, or even 40, or even 30 or even 20—but in fact there were no righteous people at all. Abraham understood it was the Lord he was conversing with. So when the Lord had finished speaking with Abraham, he left and Abraham returned to his tent.

It was evening when two angels arrived to visit Sodom. Lot was the only righteous man there, and he urged them to stay with him. They did stay, and when the people of the city, young and old, surrounded the house and started yelling that they wanted to do evil things with the visitors, those angels struck the people with blindness. Then the angels told Lot to hurry and gather together any relatives he had—daughters and sons-in-law—to get out of Sodom and escape to the mountains.

Only Lot's wife and two daughters fled the city with him, but as the angels were destroying the city, Lot's wife looked back to see what was happening, and she turned into a column of salt. Then Lot and his daughters went and lived in a cave in the mountains.

Danny Munkondia (Gen. 21, 25:12-18)

Isaac, Hagar, and Ishmael

Abraham and Sarah were very, very old, and people laughed at them because they still had no children, But God told Sarah she was going to be pregnant and have a son. She laughed, but the promise was true, and when the boy was born they named him "Isaac," which means "laughter." Then Sarah told Abraham to get rid of the servant girl Hagar and her growing boy Ishmael, the son of Abraham, because he will never share the inheritance with Isaac.

Abraham was worried when he heard those words from Sarah, but God said to him, "Do not be distressed for the boy and your maid servant. Just listen to what Sarah tells you. I will make that son of your maid servant into a great nation also."

Then Abraham provided Hagar with food and water and sent her off with her son, and she went into the desert of Beersheba. Hagar started crying in the desert because there was no water. Then God heard the boy crying and said to her, "Hagar, what is the problem? I have heard the boy crying. Do not be afraid. I will make your boy into a great nation." Hagar's eyes were opened and she saw a well of water and gave some for her boy to drink.

The boy grew up and lived in the desert and became an archer. He had many children who became tribal rulers with many settlements and camps. And Ishmael lived for 137 years, and then he died.

George Lupande (Gen. 22)

Abraham Tested

We see that in Abraham's old age God fulfilled his promise and gave him and Sarah the child named Isaac. At this time Abraham was a hundred years old.

Now God told Abraham to kill his only son Isaac on an altar as a sacrifice to God. What a difficult request. But without hesitating, Abraham took his son to be sacrificed. The son asked his father, "I see that you have taken all the materials for a sacrifice—the fire and the wood—but where is the lamb?"

His father replied, "God will provide."

When they reached the place, Abraham built an altar. He bound his son Isaac and put him on the altar. What a sad moment. As he was about to slay his son, the angel of God called to him from heaven, "Do not lay a hand on the boy."

Then Abraham looked, and in a thicket he saw a ram caught there. God himself had provided the sacrifice. Immediately Abraham took that animal and sacrificed it to God in place of his son Isaac. What a joyful moment. The father and the son went home rejoicing.

L. L. B. Kachinjika (Gen. 24)
Isaac and Rebekah

When Isaac grew up, Abraham said to his chief servant, "Go and get a wife for my son Isaac. Don't get one from the Canaanites, but get a wife from my country—one of my own relatives." The chief servant agreed to do this and went away with ten of his master's camels and all kinds of good things. When he reached Nahor where there was a well, he prayed to the God of Abraham to show him how to find the right woman. God showed him what to expect, so he stood near the well, watching as the women from the town came to draw water.

The first woman who came to the well was Rebekah, a granddaughter of Bethuel who was of the tribe of Abraham's brother Nahor. "Let me give you water," she said to the stranger standing there, "and I will also water all your camels," and she did. This was the sign to the chief servant that here was the chosen wife for Isaac. So he gave valuable gifts to Rebekah and asked if there was room for him to rest, for it was evening when all this took place.

Rebekah said, "We have straw and fodder for all your animals as well as plenty of room for you." While she ran to her mother's house to tell about all that had happened, the chief servant gave thanks to the God of Abraham for giving him success in this mission. When Laban the father of Rebekah heard the news, he hurried to the well and welcomed the chief servant to his home.

Food was prepared for the visitors, but the chief servant refused to eat. He said, "I will not eat until I have said what my master has sent me to tell you." He told about Abraham's desire to find a wife for his son Isaac, and it was agreed that the chief servant should take Rebekah with him to become the wife of Isaac. The chief servant took out the many gifts he had brought and gave them to Rebekah's family members. Then he took Rebekah to Canaan.

So the chief servant told Isaac all that had happened, and Isaac took Rebekah as his wife. He loved her, and she comforted him when his mother died.

George M. Chikoya (Gen. 23, 25:1-11)

Death of Sarah; Death of Abraham

Sarah was the first wife of Abraham. She was 127 years old when she died. She died in Hebron in the land of Canaan. Abraham went to mourn for Sarah and weep over her. Then he rose from beside his dead wife and spoke to the Hittites to say, "I am an alien and a stranger among you. Sell me a burial site so that I can bury my dead."

They had great respect for him and said they would give him the choicest of their tombs, the cave of Machpelah and the field with it. But Abraham asked the price of the field and Ephron replied, "My Lord, the land is worth 400 shekels of silver, but what is that between you and me? Bury your dead."

Abraham agreed to those terms and weighed out for him the price he had named, using the weights of the merchants. So the field in Machpelah near Mamre with all its trees and the cave in it became the property of Abraham, and he buried his wife Sarah in the cave.

Abraham took another wife whose name was Keturah. She bore him six children, and these children bore yet other children. While he was living he gave gifts to all of his offspring and sent them away, but when he died, Abraham left everything he owned to his oldest son, Isaac.

Abraham lived for 175 years, then breathed his last at a good old age. His sons Isaac and Ishmael buried their father in the cave of Machpelah near Mamre in the field of Ephron where his wife was buried, and God blessed Isaac after his father Abraham died.

Ronald Chinkonde (Gen. 25:19-34; 27:1-40)

Jacob and Esau

Isaac was 40 years old when he took Rebekah to be his wife. It happened that the wife was barren for some time, yet the day came when she felt some strange things in her womb. She asked the Lord what it was. God said, "Two nations are within you. The younger will be stronger than the older, and the elder will serve the younger."

The time of delivery came and she gave birth to twin boys. The first had red hair on his body like a garment, and he was called Esau. The second came out with his hand grasping his brother's heel and he was called Jacob. These boys grew up and Esau was a skilled hunter while Jacob was interested in living in tents.

After many years the time came when the father was about to die because of old age. He told his beloved son Esau to hunt game for him, prepare a savory meal of his favorite meat, and get ready to receive the blessing of the oldest son.

The mother heard these instructions and quickly told her beloved son Jacob to hurry and prepare two young goats as a meal for his father, and to bring the very important supplies of wine and bread. She also helped him to put the skins of animals on his hands and neck so that he would feel like his hairy brother Esau in case his father should touch him.

So Jacob went to his father first and received the blessing meant for the oldest son. When Esau arrived with his food, the father realized he had been deceived, but it was too late. He had already eaten a delicious meal, and already given away the blessing. Esau cried bitterly and forced his father to bless him, but his father gave him only a small blessing.

From this time forward the twin brothers Jacob and Esau were enemies.

MacDonald Chikankheni (Gen. 28)

Jacob's Blessing and Dream

Isaac blessed his son Jacob and commanded him not to marry a Canaanite woman, and he blessed him with these words: "May Almighty God bless you and make you fruitful and increase your numbers until you become a community of people. May he give you and your descendants the blessings promised to my father Abraham so that you may inherit the land you now live in as an alien." Then he sent Jacob on his way to look for a wife.

Jacob was heading for Haran, and when he reached a certain place he stopped for the night because the sun had set. Exhausted from so long a journey, he took a stone and placed it under his head, and he lay down to sleep.

In that sleep he had a dream: a stairway was resting on the earth and its top reached heaven. Angels of God were going up and down this stairway, and above it stood God who said, "I am the God of your fathers Abraham and Isaac. I will give you the land where you are lying, and your descendants will spread and be a blessing among all the people. I will bring you back to this land and never will I leave you alone."

Jacob was afraid when he awoke and he said, "Surely this is the house of the Lord, the gateway to heaven." He took the stone under his head and set it up as a pillar and called that place Bethel. "If God will take care of me until I return," he vowed, "I will build his house at this place and worship him by giving one tenth of all that is mine."

Blessings M. Chagomerana (Gen. 32-33)

Jacob and Esau Reunited

Jacob became very wealthy, and when the time came to return with his wives and all his possessions to his homeland, he sent messengers to his brother Esau, asking for favor. But Esau sent them back saying he was coming to meet him, and that he had 400 people with him.

Jacob became very fearful and distressed and he prayed to God to find out what to do. After praying, he decided to do this: He divided those things he had into groups and sent one group with gifts for his brother on ahead, and he himself spent the night in the camp. He also sent his wives across the river to go ahead, along with his possessions.

When Jacob was alone, a man wrestled with him until daybreak. Jacob would not let him go, so the man touched the socket of Jacob's hip in a way that stopped him from wrestling, and there the man blessed him. So Jacob called that place Peniel, the place where he wrestled with God.

After that Jacob saw his brother Esau coming, so he bowed down seven times before him and all his people did the same. But Esau hugged and kissed his brother and showed great feelings of joy. So Jacob gave many gifts to his brother and insisted that he accept it. Then Esau returned to Edom and Jacob went to Shechem.

Nelson Banda (Gen. 37)

Joseph's Dreams / Sold into Slavery

Jacob was a most successful man with many possessions and four wives, yet the trouble was with his most beloved wife, Rachel, who was not getting pregnant. Finally she was able to have that baby Joseph, and then she died in childbirth after delivering that second son, Benjamin. That is why, although Jacob had 12 sons, Joseph and Benjamin were special.

So Jacob gave his favorite son Joseph a very colorful robe, and having that robe aggravated the already strained relations between Joseph and his 10 older brothers. Joseph then fueled the fire by telling his strange dreams.

"We were binding sheaves in the field," he told his brothers, "and your sheaves were bowing down to mine!" But they hated him and scoffed at the idea that he would reign over them.

"I had another dream!" he announced. "This time, the sun, the moon, and eleven stars bowed down to me."

Even his father rebuked him for that one. "Do you really think that I and your mother and your brothers will bow down to you?" So Jacob sent his boy out to find his brothers who were tending sheep.

When they saw him coming the older brothers said, "Here comes that dreamer!" and they ripped away his cloak and threw him into a pit. Later some traders with camels came that way and his angry brothers sold him as a slave to get rid of him.

They dipped the robe in blood and showed it to their father who assumed his beloved son was dead, perhaps killed by some wild animal.

McPherson Banda (Gen. 39-40)
Prison Dreams
Those traders took Joseph to Egypt and sold him as a slave to one of Pharaoh's officials known as Potiphar who was captain of the security forces there. He was such a good slave that Potiphar put him in charge of everything he had, but the problem was with Potiphar's wife.

Joseph was very handsome, and Potiphar's wife cast longing eyes upon him saying, "Come to bed with me." Finally she tried to pull him into her bedroom. Joseph refused her advances and escaped, but not before she had pulled off his outer garment.

When she saw she could not get what she wanted, she caused a great commotion and deceived her husband by telling him that Joseph had tried to take advantage of her. In great wrath the master sent Joseph to prison.

Even in prison God was with Joseph. Soon he was put in charge of the other prisoners. One day the man who was cupbearer to the king was put in prison with Joseph, and so was the baker. When those two men fell asleep, each of them dreamed a dream. They woke up and did not know what the dreams meant, so they told the dreams to Joseph.

In the dream of the chief cupbearer, a vine of three branches budded, blossomed, and produced grapes. The cupbearer squeezed the grapes into a cup and served it to Pharaoh. Joseph told him that the three branches represented three days when Pharaoh would have him resume his duties as cupbearer. And Joseph requested that the cupbearer remember him when the dream came true.

The chief baker admired what had been interpreted and decided to reveal his dream as well. He dreamed of three baskets full of bread on his head. The top basket had all kinds of good things for Pharaoh, but the birds were eating the bread out of the basket. Joseph told him that the three baskets represented three days when Pharaoh would have him hanged on a tree and the birds would eat his flesh from there.

Everything that Joseph interpreted to the chief cupbearer and the chief baker came true. However, the cupbearer forgot all about Joseph when he was restored to serving Pharaoh.

Fred Bamus (Gen. 41)

Pharoah's Dream

The day came when Pharaoh had a dream he could not understand. In this dream he was standing by the River Nile, and out of the river there came up seven cows, sleek and fat, and they grazed among the reeds. After them, seven other cows, ugly and gaunt, came up out of the Nile and stood beside those fat ones. And the cows that were ugly and gaunt ate up the seven sleek cows. Then Pharaoh woke up.

He fell asleep again and had a second dream: seven heads of grain, healthy and good, were growing on a single stalk. After them, seven other heads of grain sprouted—thin and scorched by the east wind. The thin heads of grain swallowed up the seven healthy, full heads. Then Pharaoh woke up again.

In the morning his mind was troubled, and he sent for all the magicians and wise men of Egypt. Pharaoh told them his dreams, but no one could explain to him what they meant.

Then the cupbearer remembered a dream of his own when he was in prison, and he remembered the other prisoner, Joseph, who had correctly interpreted his dream—and everything he had dreamed came true. So he told all of this to Pharaoh. Then the king told his people to quickly take Joseph out of prison and bring him in there to interpret these dreams.

"The two dreams of Pharaoh are one and the same," Joseph explained. "God has revealed to Pharaoh what he is about to do. The seven good cows are seven years, and the seven good heads of grain are seven years. It is the same dream. The seven lean, ugly cows that came up afterward are seven years, and so are the seven worthless heads of grain scorched by the east wind: they are seven years of famine. So seven years of abundance are coming to Egypt, and they will be followed by seven years of famine."

Then Pharaoh put Joseph in charge of making many preparations to store all the grain from seven years of abundance. He took his signet ring from his finger and put it on Joseph's finger. He dressed him in robes of fine linen and put a gold chain around his neck. He had him ride in a chariot as his second in command, and men shouted before him, "Make way!" Then Pharaoh put Joseph in charge of the whole land of Egypt.

Those seven good years came, and then began the seven years of famine. All the countries around came to Egypt to buy grain from Joseph. Then Pharaoh said to Joseph, "I am Pharaoh, but without your word, no one will lift hand or foot in all of Egypt." So Joseph ruled the land. This is how the dreams of Pharaoh came true.

Section 3: Migration and Return

A story from the grandmother of Hawa Phiri:
"Snake! Snake! Snake!"

My grandmother talks about the Tonga tribe, the battle between the Tonga and Ngoni, and folk tales. In her stories she always sings a song related to her story, and that makes her story interesting and good. We do not get tired of listening. She tells these stories after supper when we meet together with my children as we surround the fire. She wants us to know about things that happened before we were born, and also to make us love more stories and more folk tales. Her stories take 10 or 15 minutes. Here is one of her stories:

In our area, there was a woman who wanted to be rich. She went to the African doctor to ask his help about her plan, and he told her what she must do. He gave her medicine from trees mixed with bones from fish. He told her to go home, put her medicine in the four corners of her house, and then to wait for some days to see what will happen.

"You will see a small snake coming into your house," he told her. "But you are not to kill it until it goes away." She believed that and was ready to obey. She went home and did as the doctor said. After three days a snake came into her house while she went away to the market. The snake found her sleeping daughter and bit her on the leg. When the mother came home she found her daughter crying and the snake moving away. Confused, she tried until sunset to catch the snake, but she could not.

The daughter became sick but the mother gave her no medicine. At midnight, while the daughter was again sleeping, the snake came to the house again. But—lucky enough—the daughter woke up and starting shouting, "Snake! Snake! Snake!"

Then her mother took a stick and beat the snake until it died. The daughter died at the same time, but the mother thought she was only sleeping. She took the snake and threw it into the outhouse toilet, came back into the house and found her daughter sleeping. She called her name, but the girl didn't answer. So the mother went out and called her neighbors to come awaken her daughter, but they told her the girl was dead.

The mother sat and cried because she knew now that the medicine she received from the African doctor was not good, and that is why her daughter died. She tells openly that she did not try again to receive medicine from anyone in order to be rich. She understood now what was good and what was bad.

From that time on this woman stopped believing in magic and became a Jesus follower. She confessed her sins to God and asked him to forgive her. She remains alive until now and in her old age continues as a faithful one at church.

Hawa Phiri (Gen. 45:4-46-7)

Joseph Saves His People

Joseph's brothers came to Egypt to buy grain for there was a famine in all the land. What amazement they felt when they learned that the brother they had sold into slavery some years ago was not dead but had become the most powerful ruler in Egypt next to Pharaoh. Joseph said to his brothers, "Come close to me. I am Joseph who you sold into Egypt! Do not be afraid. And do not be angry at yourselves for selling me here. It was God's will to save me and to send me here to save you. For two years there has already been famine, and for the five years to come there will not be plowing and reaping. But God sent me here ahead of you to preserve our family on earth and to save your lives by a great deliverance. God is the one who made me like Pharaoh, lord of his entire household, and ruler of all Egypt.

"So, my brothers! Hurry back to my father Jacob and tell him that his son Joseph is still alive, and God has made him Lord of all Egypt. Come back down here to me and don't delay. You shall live in the region of Goshen and be near me. Bring your children and grandchildren, your flocks and all you have. I will provide for you in the five years of famine still to come. You can see for yourselves, and so can my brother Benjamin, that it is really I who am speaking to you."

Then Joseph threw his arms around his brother Benjamin and wept, and Benjamin embraced him weeping, and he kissed all his brothers and wept over them.

So the news reached Pharaoh's palace that Joseph's brothers had come. Pharaoh and his officials were pleased, and urged Joseph to invite his entire family to live in the best land that Egypt had to offer. "Never mind about your belongings," Pharaoh said, "because all the best of Egypt will be yours!"

When the brothers returned to Canaan and told their father this news, Jacob was not believing them. But then they showed him everything Joseph had given to them—new clothes, food and money for the journey, donkeys, grain and bread—even a cart to ride in! Then the spirit of their father Jacob revived and he said, "I am convinced!

My son Joseph is still alive! I will go and see him before I die."

So they made the journey, and when they reached a place called Beersheba Jacob offered a sacrifice to the God of his fathers, and God spoke to him in a vision at night and said, "Jacob, Jacob, I am the God of your fathers. Don't be afraid to go down to Egypt, for I will make you a great nation there. I will go to Egypt with you, and I will surely bring you back again." So Jacob left Beersheba and went to Egypt with all his family and livestock and possessions, and they lived in Egypt all through that famine.

Blessings Chagomerana (Exod. 1-3)

Moses

God gave Jacob a new name, calling him "Israel," so his 12 sons and their children came to be known as the children of Israel. When Jacob came to Egypt, he had with him 70 people, but his children, the Israelites, multiplied and filled the country more and more. Then Jacob died, and when his time came, his son Joseph also died. As the many years passed, the Israelites became a great swarm of people.

Many years passed until a new king of Egypt came to power. He did not know who Joseph was, and he told his people to oppress the Israelites and make them slaves. This did not work out well for him, because the more they were oppressed, the more the people of Israel multiplied.

These Israelites spoke a language called Hebrew, and sometimes they were called by their language. In fact, the king of Egypt told the Hebrew midwives to kill every boy child and let the girl babies live, but the midwives didn't do that. They feared God more than they feared Pharaoh. So then Pharaoh ordered that every male child of the Hebrews must be thrown into the river to drown.

One Israelite woman from the tribe of Levi—one of Jacob's 12 sons—put her newborn son into a basket before throwing him into the river, so he floated safely for three months. But when the mother could no longer hide him, she put the basket among the reeds along the Nile River where Pharaoh's daughter came to bathe, and she instructed the older sister of the baby to watch and find out what would happen.

Pharaoh's daughter found that child and knew he was a Hebrew baby. But she drew him out of the water and wondered what to do with him. Then the sister came up and asked, "Would you like me to find a woman from among the Hebrews who can nurse this baby for you?"

And that is what happened. She brought her own mother—the mother of the baby—and Pharaoh's daughter gave her the job of raising this baby! And she gave him the name "Moses," because, she said, "I drew him out of the water."

One day after he had grown up, Moses saw an Egyptian beating a Hebrew slave, so Moses killed the Egyptian and hid his body in the sand. The next day he saw two Hebrews fighting each other, so he said to one man, "Why are you fighting your fellow Hebrew?"

The man replied, "Who put you a ruler among us? Do you want to kill me as you did that Egyptian?" Then Moses saw that his secret had been revealed, so he ran away so Pharaoh could not kill him.

Moses went to Midian where he lived with a priest by the name of Jethro, who gave him a daughter called Ziporah to marry. So Moses stayed there for many years and took care of his father-in-law's flocks of animals. Meanwhile, the suffering of the Israelites back in Egypt increased and they began to cry out to God because of their slavery. So God remembered his covenant with their fathers and became concerned.

Moses was tending Jethro's flock and he came to Horeb, the Mountain of God. There the angel of God appeared to him as fire in a bush that appeared to be burning. So Moses came near, surprised because the bush did not burn up. God called Moses two times from within the bush and said, "Do not come closer—the place you are standing is holy ground."

God talked with Moses for a long time in that place. He said, "I have seen the suffering of my people in Egypt, and I hear them crying out to me. So I have come down to rescue them, and to take them to a good and spacious land that flows with milk and honey—the land that I promised to their grandfathers." Then God asked Moses to be the one to lead these people away from Egypt.

Moses wondered this: "What can I say when they ask, 'who put you a ruler among us?'"

"I Am who I Am," the Lord replied. "Tell them 'I Am' has sent you." He also told Moses that Pharaoh would not be willing to let the people go. It would take many miracles, but at the end he will let them go. Finally he said, "I Am the Lord."

Winiko Wanyetha (Exod. 11-12)

Passover and Exodus

God was right—Pharaoh would not let the Israelite slaves leave, and so God gave Moses the power to cause many plagues to trouble Egypt. Water turned to blood, frogs and lice and flies and grasshoppers filled the land. Hail and thunder shook the villages, skin boils appeared on the people, and darkness covered the earth. None of this persuaded Pharaoh to believe in a god more powerful then himself.

Finally the Lord said to Moses, "I will bring one more plague on Pharaoh and on Egypt—the angel of death. So tell my people that men and women alike are to ask their neighbors for articles of silver and gold."

Moses said to the people, "About midnight the angel of death will go throughout Egypt and all the first born sons in Egypt will die, from the firstborn son of Pharaoh who sits on the throne to the firstborn son of the poorest girl who is at her hand mill—and all the firstborn of the cattle as well."

Then Moses instructed the people on how to prepare a lamb to sacrifice in order to protect themselves from death. They were to put the blood of the lamb on the door frames of their houses, and when the angel of death saw the blood, he would pass over them and not kill the firstborn of that household.

Everything happened as God promised, and in the night Pharaoh summoned Moses and his brother Aaron and said, "Up! Leave my people, you and the Israelites.

Go! Worship the Lord your God as you have requested. Take everything you have and go—and also bless me."

The Israelites did all that Moses instructed, and they carried great wealth with them as they left that land of slavery. That is why, on that night each year, the Israelites are to keep vigil and celebrate Passover to honor the Lord in all the generations to come, for the angel of death has passed over them.

George Lupande (Exod. 19:20-20:21; Exod. 34: 29-35)

Ten Orders

When the Israelites came out of Egypt, God called Moses to receive ten instructions—orders that he and all the people must follow. There were ten of them:

1. You shall have no other gods before me
2. You shall not make yourself an idol in the form of anything in heaven or on earth
3. You shall not misuse the name of the Lord
4. Remember the Sabbath
5. Honor your father and mother so that you may live long
6. You shall not murder
7. You shall not commit adultery
8. You shall not steal

9. You shall not give false testimony against your neighbor
10. You shall not desire your neighbor's house, or his wife, or his servants, or his ox, or donkey, or anything else that belongs to your neighbor.

When Moses was coming from Mount Sinai where God gave him the two tablets with the ten instructions carved into them, he was a changed man in the appearance of his face. His face became radiant just because he had spoken with God. His brother Aaron and all the Israelites were afraid, so Moses put a veil over his face so that he might be together with his people.

P. Alufasi Phiri (Exod. 39:32-40:38)

The Tabernacle

On their way to the land of promise, the children of Israel lived for many years in tents in the desert. A time came when God gave them instructions for building a special tent of worship—a tabernacle. So when the Israelites completed the work on the tabernacle and the tent of meeting, they brought it to Moses along with all the furnishings.

Furnishings included woven garments for the priests to wear in the sanctuary, both sacred garments for Aaron the priest and garments for his sons when serving as priests. Then God blessed his people because they made everything exactly as he had instructed them.

God told Moses to set up the tabernacle on the first day of the first month, and to place a special chest called an ark inside. This holy place was shielded by a curtain made for that purpose. They brought in the chest and set out what belonged on it, and put everything needed into the tabernacle.

Then God told Moses to take the anointing oil and touch the tabernacle with it; sprinkle oil on every sacred thing. Devote it and all its furnishings to God so it will be holy. Also, anoint the altar of burnt offering and all its tools. Make the altar to be most holy. Then place the altar of burnt offering and the basin of water in the front of the entrance, and set up the courtyard around it and the curtain at the entrance to the courtyard. Finally, he told them to dress Aaron and his sons in the sacred garments and anoint them to be a priesthood that will continue for all generations.

When everything was done exactly as God instructed, a cloud covered the tent of meeting and the glory of the Lord filled the tabernacle. In all the travels of the Israelites, whenever the cloud lifted from above the tabernacle, they would set out and follow the cloud. When the cloud did not move, than they also did not move. So the cloud of the Lord was over the tabernacle by day and fire was in the cloud by night in the sight of all the people of Israel during all their travels.

Danny Munkondia (Deut. 8-9:5)

Do Not Forget the Lord

Do you remember how the Lord led you through the desert for 40 years? God humbled you, causing you to hunger and then feeding you with manna. He taught you that man does not live on bread alone but on the word of God as well. God provided you with everything during those 40 years. The Lord disciplined you just as a man does for the son he loves.

Consider God's command of walking in his ways and respecting him. God is bringing you into a good land—a land with streams and pools of water, with springs flowing in the valleys and hills; the land with wheat, barley, vines, and fig trees. Praise the Lord your God for the good land he has provided for you.

Be careful that you do not forget the Lord. Otherwise, when you eat and are satisfied and build fine houses and settle down, and when your possessions become large and your silver and gold increase, then your heart will be proud and you will forget the Lord your God who brought you out of slavery in Egypt to this land of plenty.

Do not be proud. Remember that the Lord is the one who gives you the ability to produce wealth. You will be destroyed if you forget the Lord and follow other gods. You will also be destroyed for not obeying the Lord.

Israel, now you are about to cross the Jordan River to go in and own the land of the tall and strong Anakites. Who can stand against them? But know for sure that the Lord is the one who goes in front of you like a devouring fire. He will destroy them because the land is promised to you.

After the Lord has done all things, don't say to yourself, the Lord has given me these possessions because of my own goodness. No! It is because of the wickedness of these nations that the Lord will drive them out before you. So go out and accomplish what he swore to your forefathers, to Abraham, Isaac, and Jacob.

George M. Chikoya (Deut. 28)

Blessings for Obedience

Let me tell you some of the rewards we will be given once we obey God. These are the blessings of obedience: Your city and country will be blessed; your land and your young livestock will be blessed; the fruit from your womb will be blessed.

What a wonderful Lord he is, making even your basket and kneading trough worthy to be blessed because of your obedience. When walking up and down, here and there, blessings will follow you, in and out, wherever you go.

What is left to tell of how God will bless you? When enemies rise against you, it is the Lord's will to protect you. What about your barns? It is also his desire to bless them. But the great blessing is that you will be able to call on the name of the Lord, the Holy One.

Oh my marvelous Lord, how wonderful you are.

Lemiter Kachinjika (Josh. 23-24:31)

Joshua's Farewell and Death

After a long time had passed and the Lord had given Israel rest from all their enemies, Joshua was old and advanced in years. So he gathered all the Israelites and reminded them what God did to other nations who were citizens of these lands of Canaan. God removed the nations and gave Israel their land.

Joshua also warned against worshiping the gods of those nations because God judged them for this great sin. Joshua said to never associate with those gods, invoke their names, or even swear by them. He said that if the Israelites do what Joshua says, they will be able to defeat any remaining nations that were like traps for them, or whips on their backs, or thorns in their eyes.

Joshua warned them not to violate God's covenant, for if they do this, then God will destroy them completely. Then Joshua said, "This is my time to die."

After this first assembly, Joshua held another to explain what happened in the time from Abraham to Moses, and how God did everything for them and made important promises for their descendants. Joshua also explained how God led them out of Egypt, through the wilderness, and up to now. He instructed them on how to take over the leadership after he died.

Joshua explained to the people what their forefathers worshipped beyond the river and in Egypt, and he gave them a choice: either worship and serve the gods of their forefathers, or worship the God of heaven and earth. The people of Israel agreed to choose to serve the Lord because it was the Lord who brought them out of slavery in Egypt.

Finally, Joshua warned the people that if they serve other gods, then God will punish them. Then Joshua removed all the gods from among the Israelites and he wrote down the covenant he made with them in the book of the law.

McPherson Banda (1 Sam. 17:1-54; 18:6-8)

David and Goliath

People called Philistines were fighting against God's people, Israel, and they were trusting in their weapons to save them. They were also a people who had giants, and their champion of war—Goliath—walked in front of them. The Israelites under King Saul assembled for war in the Valley of Elah, and they were trusting in their God to save them.

Goliath started to insult and defy the Israelites by promising to hurt them in many ways. For 40 days he did this before the war started. These insults made the Israelites to be dismayed and terrified. None of the Israelites managed to withstand the situation except the young boy David with his sling and five stones. He trusted in God.

Even though Goliath insulted them and acted big, the boy David came to the front of the battle, put a stone in his sling, and powerfully flung that rock into the forehead of Goliath. When that giant fell to the ground, David ran to him, took that big man's own sword, and used it to cut off the giant's head. Then all the Philistines ran away before the armies of Israel who saw that God was saving them by the courage and obedience of that boy David.

The women of Israel celebrated this victory by making a song: "Saul has killed his thousands, but David his ten thousands," so that is how the spreading of this joyful news made King Saul jealous and angry.

Chifundo Patrick (2 Sam. 5:1-16)

David Becomes King

When David was first anointed king, Samuel did this privately, first making David king just over the tribe of Judah. So after King Saul died, the people of Israel came to David and said, "We are your own flesh and blood, and even when Saul was king, you were the one who led Israel on our military campaigns. The Lord has said to you, you will shepherd my people Israel." So they anointed David to be their king when he was 30 years old, and he reigned for 40 years.

Before this time, David was forced to live as an outlaw and life looked bleak, for Saul was trying to kill him because of great jealousy. But God's promise to make David king over all Israel was now being fulfilled. The people loved David so much because he was strong in his heart.

David became more and more powerful because the Lord Almighty was with him all of his life. He built a residence in the city of David, which was Jerusalem, and also King Hiram of Tyre sent messages to David along with cedar logs and carpenters and stonemasons, and they built a palace for David.

David wrote many songs and poems, and with those words he encouraged his people to live for God. Here is one of his sayings:

> Blessed is the man
> Who does not take
> Advice from the wicked.
> Or stand with sinners
> Or sit with mockers.
> But his delight is in
> The law of the Lord.
> He thinks long about this law
> Both during the day and at night.

Ronald Chikonde (Ps. 8; 14:1-6; 15)

A Teaching of David

Oh Lord God, your name is wonderful.
You are king of things in heaven and earth.
Children are able to trust and praise you without doubts.
We ask you God to give us childlike faith.

Remove barriers from a good relationship with you.
When we look at creation, we often feel small.
When we look at the vast expanse,
We wonder how God could care about people—
People who often disappoint you.
Yes God, you made us lower than him and angels,
But we have great worth because
We bear the stamp of the creator.
God gave us tremendous authority,
We are in charge of the whole earth.
God honored us greatly and gave us responsibility.
Praise to God! We appreciate his worth.

Psalm 15:1-5

Lord God Almighty, who may stand in your righteous presence? Our standards for living should not come from our evil society. The one who fears the Lord humbles himself before the throne of the glory of God.

We have to live by the standard of the Lord. God honors those who say the truth and in their mouths there is nothing deceitful. Words are powerful; we must use them well. The Lord wants us to love one another with love that sets no limits. Loving like this honors the Lord.

The people who fear the Lord and walk his ways—no matter what the situation is—those people who don't love because of gain, but those who have true love, they are the ripe fruit.

They are the people who don't make unfair profits or loans to the needy, who treat innocent people accordingly.

Everyone who loves the Lord and puts his trust in him is like the Mount of Zion which is not shaken—forever!

MacDonald Chikankheni (2 Chron. 7:11-27)
Solomon, Son of David

When King David died, his son Solomon became king in his place. He went right to work building the Lord's temple and furnishing it with all the things necessary there, carefully following all the instructions of the Lord.

After finishing this work, the Lord appeared to him saying, "Solomon, I have heard your prayers and from today this place is mine as well as the temple of sacrifice. I am the only one who makes the rains to come on the earth. I can harm the land and even the people.

"But if my people, called by my name, repent of their sins and return to me, then I will forgive their sins and heal their land. Then my eyes will be open and my ears listening for their prayers offered in this place. I have set apart this place forever. Therefore, just be obedient like your father David was to me.

"However, if you forsake me for other gods, I will uproot Israel from this land. I will reject this temple and make it ridiculous among the people. They will talk about its destruction, but then they will realize it is just because you left me to worship other gods."

Fred Bamus (Prov. 1)

A Teaching of Solomon

The teachings of Solomon are given to us for attaining wisdom and discipline; for understanding words of insight. Let the wise listen and add to their learning and let the discerning get guidance. Fearing the Lord is the beginning of knowledge, but fools despise wisdom and discipline.

Other proverbs of Solomon warn against temptation. If sinners entice us, let us not give in to them or go with them. Our foot should not step in their paths because their feet rush into sin and they are swift to shed blood. Instead, we are encouraged to listen to our parents' instructions and to not forsake our mother's teaching. That wisdom is like a garland to grace our head and a chain to decorate our neck.

Do not reject wisdom. Wisdom calls aloud in the street. She raises her voice in the public squares. At the head of the noisy streets she cries out. In the gateways of the city she makes her speech. If we respond to her rebuke, she will pour out her heart to us and make wise thoughts known to us.

But since we reject wisdom and ignore her advice and do not accept rebuke, she will laugh at our disaster and mock when calamity overtakes us—when disaster sweeps over us like a whirlwind, when distress and trouble overwhelm us—then we will call, but she will not answer, we will look for her, but will not find her.

Since we hated knowledge and did not choose to fear the Lord, since we would not accept his advice and spurned his rebuke, we will eat the fruit of our ways and be filled with the fruit of our schemes. The waywardness of the simple will kill us. The complacency of fools will destroy us. But whoever listens to wisdom will live in safety and be at ease without fear or harm.

Nelson Banda (Eccles. 11-12:7)
Remember Your Creator

To remember our Creator means to obey him and follow what he says, for God created us to be with him. Remember our God for he has given us all things in order to praise him. Be happy, young man, while you are young, and keep in the way of our God, because everything belongs to our Creator.

Remember your Creator in the days of trouble because our God is peace. Thank him all the time. Blessed is the man who loves and obeys the Lord; the Lord will give him rest. Remember the Creator who provides things for us: water, food, life, and knowledge. He also gives us the sun shining in the day, and the moon at night, and the wind. Remember the Creator, for he gives us power to do works that praise him.

Remember him in all things. Fear God and keep his commandments, for this is the whole duty of man.

Billiat William (Jer. 1; 2:1-12)

God is Forgotten

One day God said to Jeremiah, "before I formed you in the womb of your mother, I appointed you to be a prophet to all the nations." But Jeremiah wanted to refuse God because he thought he was too young and could not speak well.

But God said, "Don't say that you are a child. You must go to the country where I send you, and do not be afraid because I will be with you." Then God touched Jeremiah's mouth and put the words of God there: "See?

Today you have authority over nations and kingdoms to uproot and tear down, to destroy and overthrow, to build and to plant."

After that, God appeared to ask Jeremiah a question: "What do you see Jeremiah?" Jeremiah answered that he saw the branch of an almond tree, and God said, "Yes. You answered correctly. I am watching to see that my words will be fulfilled to all the nations."

And then God said this to Jeremiah: "Get ready and say whatever I command you. Do not be terrified but be confident because I will be with you always. People will try to fight against you, but they will fail, and I will rescue you from the evil people."

After that God sent Jeremiah to the people of Israel to explain about things that did not please him. The people were following worthless idols and prophesying by Baal, and therefore God brought a charge against the people of Israel. He promised to punish them, and he sent that message to them through his prophet Jeremiah.

Section 4: Expatriates Restored

A story from the grandfather of Fred K. Bamus:

The Widow Mary Lynod

A certain woman was a widow, for her husband died about two weeks after their marriage. This was Mary Lynod, a faithful and joyful woman. Her smile could put the sun to shame even though she was childless, found work difficult, and felt lonely always. Mary Lynod lived in a small house and because of her humbleness, people in the village were jealous of her. But Mary knew that she should always rejoice even in difficult circumstances.

One day Mary bought a goat and planned to breed it so she might find help when money is gone, since she could sell the kid that would be born. She loved her goat and kept it in her house, gave it clean water, and loved it as a child. But one day her goat ate the crops from the garden of the chief. Mary was at great risk before this quick-tempered chief.

Sure enough, the chief called on Mary to say she had to leave the village. She had to go to a lonely place and live there because her goat ate his important crops.

So because the chief had authority in his village, he said the village must get rid of Mary. That same week some men volunteered to build a grass thatched house for Mary in an isolated place, and Mary accepted the command to leave.

One day, war broke into the village. Some people were killed as others ran away. The soldiers passed through Mary's poor house and felt pity and concern to see her living in the small place in a forest. They also wondered why she was not afraid. She said she was ready to die since her husband was already dead, and she had no children to worry about. Also, the chief had cast her out, so she felt unloved.

Soldiers passing through the village took a daughter of the chief, but when they saw how Mary was alone and facing difficulties without a child, they gave Mary the daughter of the chief as a helper and then continued their journey. But in the village, the chief found his daughter missing and thought she was killed by the soldiers.

The chief advertised that to anyone who found his daughter alive, he would reward that person with land and authority. Sure enough, word soon came that Mary who he had cast out into the forest was caring well for his daughter!

The chief was very happy. He told people to go and bring Mary and his daughter back home. Then the chief gave Mary land and villages—he made her chief over six villages and she became famous for wise ruling. She judged conflicts fairly and gave equal opportunity to both men and women.

We see in the life of Mary Lynod that even if we must sit through lonely places and think about difficulties, we must remember the Proverb : "No matter how long it may take, faithful people will sing praise to the Creator."

Fred K. Bamus (Jer. 3:1-18)
Unfaithful Israel

The Lord declares, "If a man divorces his wife and she leaves him and marries another man, should he return to her again? Would not the land be completely defiled? But you have lived as a prostitute with many lovers—would you now return to me?"

God has been seeing the people of Israel sitting for lovers by the side of the road like nomads in the desert. They have defiled the land with their worshipping of other gods. So, during the reign of King Josiah, the Lord said to Jeremiah, "Have you seen what faithless Israel has done?"

God thought they would soon realize other gods are helpless, and then they would return to God. But they did not return with their hearts but only in pretense. Now God calls them to return to him and he will no longer frown on them because he is merciful, but what they must do is to see and understand their guilt.

God symbolizes himself as a husband who chose us as his wife and brought us to Zion. He will give us shepherds after his own heart, shepherds who fill us with knowledge and understanding. At that time we will call Jerusalem the throne of the Lord and all nations will gather in Jerusalem to honor the Lord.

No longer will we follow the stubbornness of our evil hearts because the Lord our God is with us. Only He will be our Lord forever.

McPherson Banda (Jer. 52:1-30)
Fall of Jerusalem

Zedakiah became king and did things that in the eyes of God were very, very bad. This brought the anger of God against him. He also broke a treaty with the king of Babylon which made that king angry.

In Jerusalem there was a great famine which gave the Babylonian army a chance to break the city wall by making a hole for them to go through. They captured

Zedekiah since he had no security. His sons were killed, his eyes were blinded, and he was taken to Babylon to serve his life imprisonment.

Later, the imperial commander of the Babylonian army came back to Jerusalem and burned the temple, the royal palace, and all the houses in Jerusalem. He took away all the wealth and glory that had been there. Only poor people were left in the country to care for the vines and fields, but 4,600 people were taken at that time to serve their imprisonment in Babylon.

Nelson Banda (Lam. 1:1-22)

Sorrow for Failure

This is the prophet Jeremiah's song of sorrow because of the destruction of Jerusalem. The nation of Judah was utterly defeated, the temple destroyed, and the captives taken away to Babylon. Jeremiah's tears showed the suffering and humiliation of the people, but those tears penetrated even deeper into his heart. He wept because God had rejected the people for their rebellious ways.

Each year this book was read aloud to remind all the Jews that their great city fell because of their stubborn sinfulness. Jerusalem foolishly took a chance and lost, refusing to believe that immoral living brings God's punishment. As surely as judgment came upon Jerusalem, so will it come upon those who defy God. Obedience is the sign of your love for God.

God is the comforter, but because of the sins of the people, he had to turn away from them and become their judge. Babylon, although sinful, was God's instrument for punishing Judah and its capital, Jerusalem.

Blessings Chagomerana (Dan. 1:1-21)

Exile Begins

King Nebuchadnezzar of Babylon took some of the things from God's temple into his own temple. He also invited some boys from Israel, boys of knowledge and those who could serve in the king's house, to receive a Babylonian education. For three years they studied, served the king, and were fed by him. Some of the boys were the sons of Judah: Daniel, Hananiah, Mishael, and Azarriah. The chief official changed their names to Babylonian names that showed they were under Nebuchadnezzar's authority.

Daniel and his friends didn't want to be unclean by the foods they were being given. They begged the official about this matter, asking to have healthy vegetables and water instead of rich food. Even though the official was afraid these boys would look worse than the others, he did as Daniel suggested. For ten days he gave these boys vegetables. At the end of that time it was clear they were healthier and better looking than the others, so the official put all of the students on the same food plan.

God gave Daniel and his friends knowledge and understanding and learning. He also gave Daniel the ability to understand dreams and visions. By the end of their course of study, those young men went to be examined by the king. Among the entire graduating class, none was found to be as wise as Daniel, Hananiah, Mishael, and Azarriah. They were good in wisdom and understanding the times better than all the enchanters and magicians in his kingdom. So they served the king until the years of King Cyrus.

Psalm 137:1-6

By the rivers of Babylon
We sat and wept.
We remembered Zion
    And wept.
On the willows there
We hung up our harps
For our captors there
    Required of us…songs!

Our tormentors demanded
Songs of joy.
"Sing us one of the songs of Zion!"
    They said.
But how can we sing—
Sing songs of the Lord
In a foreign land?
    Oh! Jerusalem!
If I forget you,
Oh! Jerusalem!
May my right hand
    Forget its skill.
If I do not remember you,
Oh! Jerusalem!
May my tongue stick
    To the roof of my mouth.
On the willows there
We hung up our harps
There we sat
    And wept.

MacDonald Chikankheni (Ezek. 36:16-36)

Restoration Predicted

The Lord said to me again, "You, son of man, the reason I dispersed the Israelites among the nations was due to their bad actions—idol worship and bloodshed. But I've observed one problem with this: my name has been put to shame.

"This is what I've decided: With an intention to maintain the holiness of my name, I will bring you back to your own land. I will help you walk in my ways by giving you a new heart and my spirit to enable you to keep my decrees.

"Not only that, but also I will bring you back to your father's land, where there will be no famine for I will provide you with everything to earn a living. This will remind you of your sins and you will feel bad for your evil actions.

"Therefore, surely I will restore this land as a garden of Eden. You will be my people and I will be your God. Then all people will know that I am the Lord of restoration. I the Lord have spoken, and I will do it."

Ronald Chikonde (Joel 2:12-32)

I Will Pour Out My Spirit

God told the people of Zion to return to him while there was still time. He said they must repent with all their hearts and with fasting and tears. They were also told to rip their hearts—not their clothes—and to return to the Lord because he is gracious and compassionate, slow to anger and full of love.

Proclaim in Zion a holy fasting, a sacred gathering for the elders, the young, and even those nursing at the breast. Do it now! The bridegroom must leave his room and the bride her chamber. The priest who ministers before the Lord is to weep between the temple porch and the altar. Let them say, "Spare your people, O Lord! Don't make your inheritance an object of scorn, a swear word among the nations. Why should all those foreigners be asking, 'Where is their God?'"

But God will be jealous for his land and take pity on his people. God will reply, "I am sending you grain, new wine, and oil enough to satisfy you fully." And God will drive the northern army far from you, pushing it into a parched and barren land. God has fought for his people and has done wonderful and great things.

Don't be dismayed. Be glad and rejoice! Surely the Lord has done great things. Don't be afraid of wild animals, for the open pastures are becoming green and the trees are giving fruit. The fig tree and the vine yield riches, for God sends you abundant showers, both autumn and spring rains as before, and your threshing floor will be filled with grain and the vats overflow with new wine and oil.

The Lord will pay back the years the locusts have eaten. You will have plenty to eat until you are full, and you will praise the Lord your God who has worked wonders for you. My people will be ashamed no more and it will be known to all the people that God is there.

And after this I will pour my spirit on all people. Sons and daughters will prophesy. Old men will dream dreams; young men will see visions. I will pour out my spirit in those days even on my servants, both men and women.

And wonders will be shown in heaven and on earth—blood and fire and billows of smoke. The sun will not give its light and the moon will turn red before the coming of the great and fearful day of the Lord. And everyone who calls on the name of the Lord will be saved.

George Chikoya (Jon. 1-4)

A Sermon for Nineveh

God asked Jonah to preach at Ninevah, telling the evil people in that city of God's plan to punish and destroy them. But Jonah had no interest in saving these wicked people. Instead, he went down to Joppa and sailed toward Tarshish.

A great wind came and the ship was near to breaking. People cried out to their gods and all the goods were thrown out from the ship, yet the wind never stopped. When the owner of the ship came down to the bottom of the boat and found Jonah down there, Jonah said he was running away from the Lord. He said the storm would stop if they put him out of the boat into the sea, and it was done.

Jonah sank deeply into the waters where a big sea creature came and swallowed him. He spent three days and three nights in the stomach of that large fish! There, Jonah prayed for the Lord to save him. God commanded the fish to vomit Jonah onto dry land. And now, when God asked Jonah to go preach in Nineveh, he went!

The people fully received the message and started to repent, knowing that they had indeed lost all the presence of the living Lord. Even the king himself came to cover himself with sack cloth and ordered his people and animals not to taste any food—which is fasting—and he commanded everyone to turn away from their sins.

Jonah was not happy with God for allowing the sinners of Nineveh to receive the goodness of God. In his anger he demanded to be left to die, but God provided a vine that grew to shelter him. He was happy with this vine, but the next day it withered. The sun beat him again and he demanded death for a second time.

God said to Jonah, "Do you have a right to be angry about that vine? For just a day this is one vine, and the people of Nineveh are more than 120,000 and they have also many cattle. So should I not be concerned with that great city?"

Lemiter Kachinjika (Mal. 3:6-18)
A Conversation with God

God said, "I will send my messenger before me and he will prepare a way before me. Suddenly, the Lord you are seeking will come to his temple."

God asked, "Who will endure the day of his coming?" God said he will purify the Levites like gold and silver, and after these Levites are purified, then men will bring their offerings in righteousness. Even the offerings of Judah and Jerusalem will be acceptable.

Then God said he will draw near to Judah and Jerusalem. He will oppose sorcerers, adulterers, and perjurers who fraud laborers of their wages and those who oppress widows, the fatherless, and deprived aliens.

God rebuked the descendants of Jacob because they steal from God. How? By keeping the tithe that belongs to God. God warned them that if they do not tithe, they are cursed. Then God challenged them saying, "If you give tithe to me, I will open the floodgates of the heavens and bless you so much you will have no more room for it. And God continued with his promises. He said he will prevent pests from devouring crops of those who tithe.

Then God rebuked Judah about the harsh things they were saying against the Lord. He warned them about their blaspheming God. He said those people are arrogant evildoers who say they can prosper and be blessed even if they challenge God. But those who fear God will talk to God and he will listen. In fact, God will write a scroll concerning those who fear him and honor him, and these people will be his—they will see a distinction between the righteous ones and the wicked ones.

George Lupande (Neh. 1-2:1-10)
Returning to Jerusalem

When Nehemiah was still in exile, working in the palace of King Artaxerxes as one who brings the king his cup, he received a message from Jerusalem. His brother Hanani was concerned about the broken down wall of Jerusalem and the destruction of its gates. When he received this news, Nehemiah was very troubled and he sat down and wept. He also fasted and prayed for some days.

When King Artaxerxes saw that the face of Nehemiah was not all right, he asked him the reason of his sadness. Nehemiah explained all the troubles to the king. The king then wondered what Nehemiah was willing to do about this problem. So Nehemiah asked the king to send him back to Jerusalem.

With the help of God, Nehemiah was allowed to return to Jerusalem with permission to begin working to rebuild the city wall.

Danny Munkondia (Neh. 2-3:32)
Rebuilding the Wall

In the 20th year of King Artaxerxes, Nehemiah served the king as usual, but he had not been sad in his presence before. "Why does your face look so sad when you are not ill?" the king asked.

Nehemiah was very afraid, but he said to the king, "Why should my face not look sad when the city where my fathers are buried lies in ruin and its gate has been destroyed with fire?"

"What is it you want?" the king asked.

Nehemiah prayed to God and said, "If it pleases the king, and if your servant has found favor in his sight, let the king send me to the city in Judah where my fathers are buried so that I can rebuild it. May I also have letters to the various governors there so they will provide me with safe conduct to my destination? Then too, I would need a letter to the man in charge of the king's forest, so he will give me timbers to make beams for the gates, and for the city wall, and for the residence."

Because of the grace of God, the king granted all of these requests. So Nehemiah went to Jerusalem and secretly examined all the ruins—the gates that had been destroyed and the walls that had been broken down. When he understood everything that should be done, he went to the Jews who would be doing the work and said, "You see the trouble we are in. Let us rebuild the wall of Jerusalem and we will never be disgraced."

After that they started this good work. When some of the enemies of the Lord heard what they were doing, they mocked them. Nehemiah replied, "God will give us success." At that time all the citizens of Jerusalem did their part on the huge job of rebuilding the city wall.

Chifundo Patrick (Neh. 12:27-47)

Dedication of the Wall

When the wall of Jerusalem was dedicated, the Levites were sought out from where they lived and were brought to Jerusalem to celebrate joyfully. They sang the songs with music of cymbals, guitars, and flutes.

The singers gathered from regions around Jerusalem and came together to praise God and thank him for everything he had done. On this day they also offered great sacrifices and rejoiced because God had given them great joy. Women and children also rejoiced and the sound of celebration in Jerusalem could be heard far away.

Next, they chose men to be in charge of the tithes and offerings and contributions of first fruits brought in from all the surrounding areas. All these supplies were brought into the storerooms to provide for the Levites and priests so that the work of God could go forward.

Hawa Phiri (Ezra 1:1-8; 2:64-70)

The Plan of King Cyrus

Jeremiah the prophet had said a king named Cyrus would one day rebuild the temple. The Lord fulfilled this prediction in the first year of King Cyrus of Persia. He did this by moving the heart of King Cyrus to make this proclamation to his people: "The Lord the God of heaven has given me all the kingdoms of the earth. He has appointed me to build a temple for him at Jerusalem in Judea. The people of any place where survivors are living must provide silver, gold, livestock, and freewill offerings for this temple."

The family heads of Judea and Benjamin and the priests and Levites were moved in their hearts to prepare to build the house of God. All their neighbors helped, and King Cyrus brought out the many articles belonging to the temple of the Lord which Nebuchadnezzar had carried away to put in the temple of his god. Many, many things were brought out—5,400 in all, and all these valuable things were brought back to Jerusalem with the exiles as they returned.

The people who came up from the captivity returned to their own town and land. So the whole company numbered 42,360 besides their 7,337 servants and also men and women singers, horses, mules, camels and donkeys.

When they arrived at the house of the Lord in Jerusalem, these families gave offerings toward rebuilding the temple on its site. Each one gave based on his ability to give to the treasury for this work. Then all of these people settled into their proper places and towns.

P. Alufasi Phiri (Ezra 3:1-13; 6:13-18)
Rebuilding the Temple

When the exiles had returned and settled in their towns, the people held a large meeting in Jerusalem. They were all in agreement for Joshua and his team of partners to begin building the altar of God to sacrifice burnt offerings on it following the instructions written about this in the Law of Moses, that man of God.

Despite their fear of the people around them, they built the altar on its foundation and sacrificed burnt offerings on it to the Lord every time it was needed. This was even before the foundation of the Lord's Temple had been put into place.

Then they began to give money to the masons and carpenters, and they gave food and drink and oil to the workers from Sidon and Tyre so they could bring cedar by sea from Lebanon to Joppa. All this was authorized by King Cyrus of Persia. They all began this work in the second month after their arrival in Jerusalem. They appointed superintendents over the work. The foundations were laid by the priests in their vestments and with trumpets sounding and Levites singing to the Lord.

"He is good. His love to Israel endures forever," they sang. And all the people gave a shout of praise to the Lord. Many of the older priests and Levites and family heads who had seen the former temple wept when they saw the foundation of this temple put into place; the others shouted for joy.

The Jews continued to build and to prosper under the preaching of Haggai and Zechariah the prophets. When the day came that they finished and completed the temple, a great celebration took place. The people of Israel, the priests, the Levites, and all the returning exiles celebrated with joy the dedication of the house of the Lord.

They offered a hundred rams, 400 male lambs as sin offerings, 12 male goats—one for each tribe of Israel—and they installed the priests in their divisions and the Levites in their groups for the service of God at Jerusalem. They did everything by carefully following what was written in the book of Moses.

Winiko Wanyetha (Ezra 10:1-17)

Confession of Sin

Ezra the priest began to notice bad things going on among the exiles who had returned to Jerusalem. Some men were marrying foreign women and learning their evil ways. At the house of the Lord, Ezra started praying, weeping, and throwing himself down before

God. The Israelites gathered around him, also weeping bitterly.

Then Ezra talked to his people about confessing their sin and doing what was good before God. They agreed to everything he said, but there was a problem. It was the rainy season and they were all standing outside in the rain to talk about these problems.

"This is too big a problem," they said. "We can't take care of it in a day or two, standing out here in the rain." So they made a plan to have elders and judges in each town deal with this problem in a one-on-one way. And that is how Ezra solved the problem. They carefully sent away the foreign women who were leading the people of God down the path of sin.

Billiat William (Mic. 4:1-13)

The Mountain of the Lord

The mountain of the Lord's temple will become the chief mountain—it will be above the hills, and the people will come and say, "Let's go to the mountain of the Lord!"

The house of Jacob will teach good ways; the law will go out of Zion to the world, and the people will beat their swords into plows. Nations will no longer take up their weapons and fight against other nations.

You will be rescued from the nations who are against you, and from those who do not know the thoughts of God. The Lord will redeem you from your enemies. Everyone will stay by his own vine and be happy under his own fig tree, for the Lord will rule over the nations for ever and ever. For sure.

Section 5: Expected One—
Predictions Come True

A story from the village of Chifundo Patrick:
Ready to Be Rich

A certain man wanted to become rich, so he went to a witch doctor to get some help. "No problem," the witch doctor said. "When you arrived here, your problems became gone. What you must do is to be strong hearted and full of faith. Now, are you ready to be rich?"

"Yes sir!" the man said, so the witch doctor asked him many questions. Three times he asked the man to return, and three times he asked the same many questions. Then the witch doctor said the man must go to the graveyard about 8:00 in the evening and sleep there all night.

"About midnight," the witch doctor said, "You will see many people carrying a coffin. Welcome them and receive the coffin from them."

The man did everything just as the witch doctor had said. He went to the graveyard in the night and slept on a hump of someone dead. At about midnight he saw crowds of people dressed in white clothes and carrying a coffin on their shoulders. They were singing songs that were concerning a funeral, yet he woke up and said to himself, "This cannot be true. Where are they coming from? Let me run away from here." Then he fled away from that place as a truly crazy man.

My grandfather warned us that if we need to be rich, we must pray to God and also work hard; we should not try to get rich by the system of magic. This is true. Many people are in the troubles they are in because they want to be rich. They are killing people or harming their families by magic just to be rich.

Fred K. Bamus (Matt. 1:18-2:23)

Jesus

The woman Mary was prepared to marry Joseph when she was unexpectedly found pregnant by the Holy Spirit. Joseph was a righteous man, so when he heard this news he refused to shame her but thought maybe to leave her quietly so no one but he himself could know this thing.

When he was still thinking, the angel of the Lord appeared to him in a dream and said, "Joseph, you are the son of David and must take Mary as your wife, for the child received within her is by the Holy Spirit. She will give birth to a son and his name will be Jesus because he will rescue people from their sins, just as the prophets of the Lord have promised."

Joseph obeyed the angel and took Mary as his wife. She gave birth, and this Jesus was born in Bethlehem at a time when Herod was king of Judea. Wise men from the east who understood these things wanted to worship Jesus and followed a star to find him. In Judea they asked Herod how to find this baby who was born to be king of the Jews.

Herod was very angry when he got this news and told his officials to kill all the boy children. But the angel of the Lord gave Joseph another dream and said to take the mother and son and escape to Egypt. The angel said, "Stay there until King Herod is dead!" All these things and many others like them fulfilled what the Lord's prophets had said would take place concerning the Messiah.

When Herod died, the angel paid another visit to Joseph—this time in Egypt—and said now was the time to bring the mother and son and return to Israel, for the one who wanted to kill Jesus was dead. So they went to Galilee and found a village called Nazareth where they lived. It's true—the prophets had said he would be called a Nazarene—and so he was.

McPherson Banda (Matt. 3:1-17)

John the Baptist and Jesus

A man came along known by the name John the Baptist. The man had been prophesied by the prophet Isaiah. He was preaching in the desert of Judea telling people to repent because the kingdom of God was near.

That man used to eat grasshoppers and honey. He was wearing clothes made of camel's hair and held together by a leather belt around his waist. Many people from Jerusalem flocked to him to confess their sins. John was baptizing those people with water, but he promised them someone would come and baptize them with the Holy Spirit and fire.

One time Jesus went where John was baptizing in the River Jordan and asked to be baptized. John at first refused, yet Jesus encouraged him, saying that every word of God should be fulfilled. So John baptized Jesus, and just then heaven opened up and the Spirit in the symbol of the dove flew down and landed on Jesus. The great voice from heaven was heard saying, "This is my son whom I love. With him I am well pleased."

Nelson Banda (Matt. 4:1-11)

Temptation of Jesus

The Spirit led Jesus into the desert to be tempted by the devil. After 40 days of fasting he was very hungry when the tempter came to him and said, "If you are the son of God, tell these stones to become bread."

Jesus answered, "It is written: man does not live only on bread, but on every word that comes from the mouth of God."

Next, the devil took him to the holy city, had him stand on the highest point of the temple, and said, "If you are the son of God, throw yourself down. It is written: he will command his angels concerning you and they will not even let your foot strike a stone."

Jesus answered, "It is also written: do not put the Lord your God to the test."

Then the devil took him to a very high mountain to view all the kingdoms of the world and their splendor, and he said, "I will give you all of this if you will bow down and worship me."

Jesus answered, "Away from me, Satan! For it is written: worship the Lord your God, and serve him only."

Then the devil went away and angels came and attended Jesus.

Blessings Chagomerana (Matt. 8:1-17; 23-34)

Miracles by Jesus

When Jesus came down from the mountain, a great number of people followed him. A certain leprosy man came to Jesus and said, "If you are willing, you sure could heal me."

So Jesus healed the man. "Don't tell anyone about what happened to you," Jesus said. "Just go and tell the priest to be a testimony for them."

He went as far as Capernaum where there was a Roman military official requesting healing for his child. This man asked Jesus not to enter his house because he didn't deserve such a visit, but he asked Jesus to just speak the word and it would happen.

"I have not seen faith like this in all Israel," Jesus said. "Go back to your house, because of your faith, your son is healed. And now the salvation is breaking out on all the people of the world, not just on those who are descended from Abraham!" When Jesus reached the house of Peter, there he found Peter's mother-in-law suffering from fever. He touched her and she immediately felt much better, got up, and began to take care of him.

When Jesus wanted to sail to the other side of the lake, he was at sea with the disciples. A heavy wind blew and they were about to drown. The disciples cried out asking Jesus to save them.

Jesus was deeply sleeping, but when he woke up, he commanded the wind to stop blowing and warned the disciples about their little faith. The disciples wondered what kind of man this was that even the creation could hear and obey him.

Jesus reached the neighborhood of the Gadarenes where he met two strong men with evil spirits who cried out, "You—Son of God—have you come to torture us before the appointed time?" The demons begged him to send them into the pigs, and Jesus did. Then those pigs ran and fell into the sea. The farmers of the pigs took the news to the village and the whole community came and begged Jesus to go away.

MacDonald Chikankheni (Matt. 9:1-8; 18-34)

More Miracles

Jesus crossed over in a boat and came to his own land. Some people brought to him a paralyzed man who was lying on a mat. When Jesus saw their faith he said to that man, "Don't be afraid. Your sins are forgiven."

Some law teachers heard these words and said to themselves, "This man is blaspheming."

Knowing their minds, Jesus said, "Why do you entertain evil thoughts in your heart? Which is easier to say, 'Your sins are forgiven,' or to say 'Get up and walk'?" But to show who has power and authority on earth to forgive sins, he said to the paralyzed man, "Get up. Take your mat and go." And all the people were astonished and praised God for the authority of Jesus.

As he was doing this miracle, a ruler came to him and said, "My daughter is dead, but come with me and put your hand on her and raise her again." Jesus got up and followed him. Along the way was a woman who had bleeding in private places for about 12 years. She said in her heart, "If I only touch his robe, I will be healed." She did touch him, and everything happened just as she hoped.

Jesus felt the power go from him. He turned to look at her and said, "Don't be afraid my daughter. Your faith has healed you."

When Jesus entered the ruler's house and saw the mourners and the noisy crowd he said, "Get out of this house! The girl is not dead, but asleep." But they laughed at him. After the crowd went outside, he took the girl by the hand and she got up! This news spread everywhere.

As Jesus was walking out from that house, two people who were blind followed him shouting, "Have mercy on us, Son of David."

Jesus asked them, "Do you believe that I am able to do this?" They said yes, so then Jesus touched their eyes and said, "According to your faith let it be done to you," and they were healed. Jesus warned them not to tell anyone about what had happened, but they went and spread this news everywhere.

While they were going, some people brought to him a demon possessed man who could not speak. When Jesus rebuked the evil spirit, that man was free and all the people were amazed and said, "This is a strange thing in Israel." But the Pharisees insulted him by saying he was casting out demons by the power from the prince of demons.

Ronald Chikonde
(Matt. 4:18-22; Matt. 9:9-13; Luke 6:12-16)

Disciples of Jesus

When Jesus was walking by the lake of Galilee he met with Simon called Peter and Andrew his brother. They were throwing their nets into the lake for they were fishermen. "Follow me," Jesus said, "and I will show you how to fish for men." Instantly they left their fish nets to follow him.

As Jesus was taking dinner in the house of Matthew, many tax collectors and sinners came to eat with him. The Pharisees saw this and questioned the disciples by asking, "Why is your teacher eating with the tax collectors and sinners?"

Hearing this, Jesus said, "It's not the healthy who need the doctor but the sick, but go and learn the meaning of this: I desire mercy and not sacrifice. I did not come to call the righteous but sinners."

Jesus went to a mountain and spent the whole night praying to God. When morning came he called his disciples to him and chose twelve to be his apostles: Simon called Peter and his brother Andrew, Philip, Bartholomew, James, John, Matthew, Thomas, James the son of Alphaeus, Simon who was called Zealot, Judas the son of James and Judas Iscariot who became a traitor.

George Chikoya (Matt. 10:5-42)

Instructions for Disciples

Jesus sent out the 12 disciples to call on people and gave them many instructions:

1. Do not go among the Gentiles or enter any town of the Samaritans.
2. Go only to the lost sheep of Israel.
3. Preach this message: The kingdom of God is near.
4. Heal the sick and raise the dead. I have given freely to you; you give freely to others.
5. Do not take any gold or silver, extra clothes, or a spare walking stick, because the worker is supposed to get his food from those he serves.
6. Wherever you go, offer peace and stay with the same host as long as you are in that area.
7. If the home is deserving, let your peace rest there; if not, let your peace return to you.
8. If anyone will not welcome you or listen to your words, shake dust from your feet and leave that house.
9. Be aware of people who will betray you into the hands of your enemies.
10. Any person who endures up to the end, that person will be saved.
11. If people persecute you in their villages, escape to another village.
12. Do not fear a person who can kill the body; fear the one who can kill the soul.

13. If a person denies me in public, I will also deny him in the eyes of my Father.
14. Everyone who loves his children, mother, or father more than me is not worthy to follow me.

Lemiter Kachinjika (Matt. 5:1-26)

Teachings of Jesus

Jesus saw crowds gather, went up the side of a mountain, sat down and began to teach. "Blessed are those who are poor in Spirit," he said, "for theirs is the kingdom of heaven. Blessed are those who mourn—they will be comforted. Blessed are the meek—they will inherit the earth. Blessed are those who hunger and thirst for righteousness—they will be filled. Blessed are the merciful—they will be shown mercy. Blessed are the pure hearted—they will see God. Blessed are the peacemakers—they will be called sons of God. Blessed are the persecuted because of their righteousness—theirs is the kingdom of God.

"Blessed are you when people insult and persecute you and say false things about you—rejoice and be happy because great is your reward in heaven, for in the same way they persecuted the prophets."

Jesus said to his disciples, "You are the salt of the earth—but salt is useless if it loses its saltiness! How can it get salty again? It is no longer good for anything but to be thrown out and walked on like regular dirt."

Jesus said again, "You are the light of the world. A city on a hill cannot be hidden. People don't light a lamp to hide it under a bowl. Instead, they put it on a stand so it can give light to everyone. In the same way, let your light shine so all people can see your good deeds.

"I did not come to abolish the law," Jesus explained. "I came to fulfill it. I tell you the truth: until heaven and earth disappear, not one small letter of the law will disappear. Everything God has planned will be accomplished. Any lawbreaker who teaches others the same will be least in the kingdom of heaven; anyone who practices and teaches the law will be great in the kingdom of heaven." Yet Jesus assured them that without righteousness from God, they will never enter the kingdom of heaven at all.

"Do not murder," says the law, but the person angry with his brother is subject to the same judgment, and calling someone a fool puts you in danger of the fire of hell. So get right with your brother before bringing gifts to the altar! Settle matters quickly before that one you are quarreling with delivers you to the judges and rulers who can throw you into prison where you cannot escape until you have paid the last kwacha. These are truly the teachings of Jesus.

George Lupande (Matt: 5:27-48)
Teachings of Jesus 2

Jesus told his followers, "You have heard it said, 'do not commit adultery.' But I'm telling you, anyone who looks at a woman lustfully has already committed adultery with her in his heart. If any part of your body makes you sin, throw it away rather than have your whole body thrown into hell."

About divorce, Jesus said it is only permitted for the reason of marital unfaithfulness. If you divorce her for your own reason you cause her to become an adulteress as anyone who marries the divorced woman commits adultery.

Jesus spoke very strictly about oaths when he said, "Do not swear at all—either by heaven because that is the throne of God, or by earth because that is his footstool. The best way is to just say 'yes' or 'no.'"

About getting even against people who harm you in any way, Jesus said, "It is not good to resist an evil person. Your ancestors said to take an eye for an eye and a tooth for a tooth, but I say we should not take revenge. If someone hits you on the right cheek, give him an equal chance to hit you on the left cheek. Give to the one who asks and do not turn away the one who wants to borrow from you."

Loving our enemies is the other good thing. It is not enough to love just our neighbors and hate our enemies. We need to pray for those who persecute us as the God of heaven causes his sun to rise on both the evil and good; he causes his rain to fall on both the ones who do justice and the ones who cheat. Jesus said we are to be perfect, just as our heavenly Father is perfect.

Danny Munkondia (Matt. 6:1-18)

Teachings of Jesus 3

Be careful about doing your act of right things before men to be seen by them. If you do that you are not going to be rewarded by your father in heaven. If you are giving to the needy, do not announce it like hypocrites do, that you should be honored. If you are giving something, your left hand should not see what your right hand does, for your giving must be a secret. Your father who sees secrets will reward you.

When you pray, do not be like hypocrites who like to pray standing in worship centers and at corners of streets to be seen by people. For sure, they have already been rewarded in full. But when you pray to God who is unseen, go in the room and pray. Your father who sees secrets will reward you.

Do not keep babbling like pagans when you pray, for your father knows what you need before you ask him. When you pray, pray like this: "Our Father in heaven, hallowed be your name. Your kingdom come, your will be done on earth as it is in heaven; give us today our daily bread. Forgive us our debts as we also have forgiven our debtors. And lead us not into temptation but deliver us from the evil one."

Chifundo Patrick   (Matt. 6:19-34)

Teachings of Jesus 4

"Do not look somber as the hypocrites do when you fast. I'm telling you the truth: they have received their rewards in full. You should put oil on your head and wash your face so men will not know you are fasting. Your Father who is unseen will see what is done in secret will reward you.

"First, seek the kingdom of heaven and then all things will be given. Stop thinking about the treasures of the earth; lend your thoughts to the treasures to heaven where ants will not damage and robbers will not take away.

"Do not keep your treasure on earth, where many things will destroy what thieves do not steal. Just as a servant cannot serve two masters at once—he will love one and not the other—so you cannot serve both God and the earthly treasure. Your heart will stay with your treasure.

"Don't worry about your life—what to eat, what to wear, what to drink. See the birds? They do not farm. They do not store up food. God feeds them, and you are worth more than birds! First of all, go looking for his kingdom and the rest will be given to you as well.

"Your Father in heaven will forgive you if you forgive others. If you do not forgive men's sins, your heavenly Father will not forgive you."

Hawa Phiri (Matt. 7:1-23)

Teachings of Jesus 5

About judging others, Jesus said not to. If you make yourself a judge, you too will be judged. About that speck of dust in your brother's eye, he said, how will you get out that speck while in your own eye there is a plank? First, remove that plank of yours, and then you can see to get out that brother's speck.

Do not give dogs what is sacred. Do not throw pearls to pigs—they will only trample them under their feet and then turn and tear you to pieces. Ask and it will be given to you, knock and the door will be opened, seek and you will find.

Jesus wanted to know, which of you, if your son asks for bread, will give him a stone? Or if he asks for a fish, will give him a snake? So what about your Father in heaven? If you evil ones know how to give good gifts, how much more Him!"

Then too, there is that narrow gate and that wide gate. The narrow one is hard to get through, yet it leads to the kingdom of heaven. That wide gate is easy enough, yet it opens the way to hell.

And Jesus warned about false prophets. Watch out for them! They come in sheep's clothing but for sure they are wolves. By their fruit you will recognize them. Do not pick the fruit of the false prophets, but the good trees bear good fruit. A good tree cannot bear bad fruit, and every tree with no good fruit is cut down and burned. It is not you who say "Lord, Lord," who are going into the kingdom of heaven, but only he who does the will of the Father in heaven.

What about those who say, "But Lord! In your name I prophesied and in your name I drove out demons and performed miracles!"

Jesus will tell them plainly, "I never knew you. Away from me evildoers."

P. Alufasi Phiri (Matt. 13:1-23)

Parable: The Sower

Jesus told many meaningful stories. One time he said a farmer went out to sow his seed. As always happens, some of the seed fell along the path and birds came and ate it up. Some fell on shallow soil where it sprang up quickly, but when the sun came up, the plants were scorched and withered because they had no root. Other seed fell among thorns which grew up and choked the plants. Still other seed fell on good soil where it produced a crop—a hundred, sixty, or thirty times more.

The disciples came to him and asked, "Why do you tell so many stories to the people?"

He answered, "The knowledge of the secrets of the kingdom of heaven has been given to you, but not to them. Whoever has will be given more and he will have plenty. Whoever does not have, even what he has will be taken from him. This is why I speak to them in parables.

"I'm telling you, many prophets and righteous men longed to see what you see, but did not see it, and hear what you hear, but did not hear it. When anyone hears the message about the kingdom and does not understand it, the evil one comes and snatches away what was sown in his heart. This is the seed that fell along the path.

"The one who receives the seed that fell on shallow soil is the man who hears the word and at once receives it with joy. But since he has no root, he lasts only a short time. When trouble and persecution come because of the word, he quickly falls away.

"This one who received the seed that fell among thorns is the man who hears the word, but he worries about life and is deceived by wealth, so that chokes the seed, making it unfruitful.

"But the one who received the seed that fell on good soil is the man who hears the words and understands. He produces crops, yielding a hundred, or sixty, or thirty more than what was sown."

Winiko Wanyetha (Matt. 13:24-30; 36-43)

Parable: The Weeds

Jesus said to his followers that the kingdom of God is like a man who sowed wheat seeds into his field. But on a dark night when everyone was sleeping his enemies came and sowed weeds among the wheat. Therefore, when the servants went to the field they found that when the wheat sprouted and formed heads, the weeds appeared also.

The farm workers asked the owner if they should pull up the weeds and he said, "You may not do that! While you are pulling the weeds you may root up the wheat with them. Let them grow together until the harvest. At that time I will tell the harvesters first to collect the weeds and tie them into bundles to be burned. Then gather the wheat and bring it into my barn."

The disciples asked him to explain about this parable and he said, "The one who sowed good seed is the son of man, and the field is the world, and the good seeds stand for the sons of the kingdom. The weeds are the sons of the evil one and the enemy who sowed them is the devil. The harvest is the end of the age and the harvesters are the angels.

"As the weeds are pulled up and burned in the fire, so it will be at the end of the age. The son of man will send out the angels, and they will weed out of his kingdom everything that causes sin and all who do evil. He will throw them into the fiery furnace where they will be gnashing their teeth. Then the people who are the good seed will shine like the sun in righteousness in the kingdom of my Father. You have ears, so listen carefully to what I have said."

Billiat William (Matt. 13:31-35; 44-52)

Parable: Seeds and Yeast

Jesus explained to the people about the kingdom of God. He said the kingdom is like the mustard seed that was planted by a certain man. That very small seed— smaller than maize or ground nuts—when it grows up bears the leaves of a tree greater than any other seeds the man put in his garden.

And also, Jesus told the people about a certain woman who put some yeast in three measures of the flour. The wonderful thing happened: all that flour expanded.

All these things Jesus said in stories with a meaning. He himself never spoke to them without using a parable so that every prediction about him would come true. He opened his mouth with parables to reveal the hidden things of God.

Then Jesus continued to explain with yet another story. He said one man found hidden treasure, and because of his strong love for it he sold all he had and bought that field so the treasure could belong to him.

Jesus also said the kingdom of God is like a business man who looks for fine pearls. When he finds that one choice pearl, he sells everything he owns in order to buy that greatly expensive pearl.

Jesus said the kingdom of God is like a fishing net thrown into the lake, gathering together all kinds of fish. When that net is full, they pull it out of the water and start to select the fish. The good fish get thrown into the basket and the bad get thrown into the bush. He said it will be the same way at the end of the age when angels will come and choose out the wicked ones to be thrown into the lake of fire where they will cry bitterly and crush their teeth.

When Jesus finished explaining these things he asked, "Are you understanding this?"

All the people said "Yes!" Then Jesus said that the teacher of the law who has been instructed about the kingdom of heaven is like the owner of a house who brings out of his storeroom new treasures as well as old.

Section 5 B: Expected One—
Saving the People

A story from the grandfather of George Lupande:

The Nomad Chief

Long ago a great chief lived in the tents together with his people. They were nomads who moved from one place to another. One night a bodyguard of the chief told him some people were stealing food from the reserving tents. The chief gathered all the people and gave them the law that if anyone was found stealing food, he would be whipped with 40 whippings out in public.

Three days later the bodyguard told the chief that the thief had been caught. Immediately the chief went straight to the place and became very sad when he saw it was his own mother caught stealing. Everyone was silent as they watched to see what the great chief would do. Would he allow his mother to be whipped, or would he break the law?

"If I break the law and leave my mother unpunished, I will lose my respect," he said in his heart. Suddenly he removed his clothes and invited the guards to give to him the punishment supposed to be given to his mother. He was whipped to the point of death.

When this chief lived to recover from the severe whipping, he became very famous for his kindness and love in taking the punishment of his mother.

Fred K. Bamus (Matt. 14:1-21)

John Beheaded

Herod, the Roman governor of that region, arrested John the baptizer, tied him up, and put him in prison. This was because John had been telling Herod it was not lawful for him to have for himself his brother Phillip's wife, Herodias. So Herod wanted to kill John. The problem was the people, because they called John a prophet, and Herod was afraid of them.

On Herod's birthday the daughter of Herodias danced in a pleasing way for them. Herod liked this so much he promised to give her anything at all. She asked her mother for a recommendation on what to say and then said, "Give me here on a platter the head of John the Baptist."

Now Herod had sworn an oath in front of all those dinner guests that he would grant any request, so he gave the order. John was beheaded in prison and the head brought on a platter to the girl, who carried it to her mother. John's disciples came to bury the body and then went to tell Jesus this news.

Jesus heard their report, then went in private to a solitary place. But he could not escape the crowds that followed him, so he felt sorry for them and healed the sick ones. At evening, the disciples said, "It's getting late and this is a remote place. Our suggestion is that you send these people away to the villages where they can buy bread."

Jesus said, "They don't need to go away. You give them something to eat."

They answered, "We have only five loaves of bread and two fish!"

"Bring them to me," Jesus said. He invited all the people to sit down on the grass, then took the food and gave thanks for it as he looked up into heaven. Then he began to divide the food and give it to his disciples, who handed it to the people. All of them ate and were satisfied, and the disciples picked up twelve basketfuls of leftovers. About 5,000 men, besides women and children, ate this bread and fish.

McPherson Banda (Matt. 16:13-28)

Messiah must Die

When Jesus went to the neighborhood of Caesarea Philippi, he wanted to know how much people knew about him. People responded to the question with various answers. Some said he was John the Baptist come back from the dead, some said Elijah, but still others said he was Jeremiah. Then Jesus wanted to know from the disciples what they themselves believed about him.

Simon Peter was quick to give an excellent answer because he confirmed the he was the Christ, Son of the living God. The answer pleased Jesus, saying this was a revelation through the mouth of Peter from God the father.

Then Jesus spoke mysteriously, saying, "You are Peter, and on this rock I will build my church, and gates of hades will not stand against it. I will give you keys to heaven's kingdom. What you bind here will be bound there, and what you cut loose here will be loose there."

After these things Jesus started to predict his sufferings and death which will be done to him by the elders, priests, and teachers of the law. But he also promised to rise from the dead after three days.

Peter rebuked him by saying it will never happen. This comment deeply disappointed Jesus because this belief was a stumbling block to him. "Get behind me, Satan!" he said. "You do not have God's thoughts in mind, but only man's."

Jesus confirmed to his disciples that if anyone would come after him, he should first of all deny himself and take up his cross every day and follow him. He encouraged them that whoever loses his life for Jesus will find it, but whoever wants to save his life will lose it. He warned the disciples not to be addicted to the world cravings because he still rewards people according to what they have done.

Nelson Banda (Matt. 18:1-14; 19:13-15)

Who is Great?

"Who is greatest in the kingdom of heaven?" the disciples asked Jesus.

He called a little child and had him stand among them. "I tell you the truth," he said, "unless you change and become childlike, you will never enter the kingdom of heaven. You must humble yourself as this child is humble to be great. When you welcome such a one, you welcome me, and if anyone causes a little one to sin, it would be better for him to be drowned in the sea with a heavy millstone tied around his neck!

"Woe to the world because of things causing people to sin. If your hand or foot causes you to sin, cut it off. If your eye makes you sin, gouge it out. Choose to enter life maimed or crippled rather than be thrown whole into the lake of fire and hell."

Some people brought little children to Jesus to place his hands on them and pray. The disciples refused them until Jesus said, "Let the little children come to me, and do not hinder them, for the kingdom of heaven belongs to such as these."

Blessings Chagomerana (Matt. 21:33-45)

Parable of Tenants

Jesus liked to tell stories in the temple as a good way to teach people important truths about God. One day he said to them, "Someone had a vineyard and rented it to some farmers and went away. When harvest time came, he sent servants to collect his fruit, but the farmers captured these agents of the owner. They beat one, killed another, and stoned the third.

"Other servants were also sent and received the same treatment. At last the owner sent his son. The farmers recognized him as the future owner and thought to kill him so the vineyard could belong to them. And they killed him indeed. So, what do you think the owner will do to those farmers when he returns?"

The listeners said, "Those wretches will be brought to a wretched end, and the owner will rent the land to honest farmers who will share with him the harvest."

Jesus said, "Yes. The stone the builders reject becomes the capstone. And the kingdom of God will be taken from you and given to others who will produce fruit."

You see, he was a prophet, yet the Pharisees did not like this story—they knew he was talking about them.

MacDonald Chikankheni (Matt. 25:31-46)
Sheep and Goats

We have heard what Jesus did. He healed people, forgave sins, walked on the sea, and said he will come again. Now, what will he do when he returns?

When Jesus comes with all the angels in his glory, he will sit on the throne and gather all the nations before him. Then he will separate people one from another, some to the right and the others to the left. Then he as king will say to those on his right, "Come, you blessed by my Father, and inherit the kingdom of God for all the good things you did on the earth to other people. You fed the hungry, gave a drink to those who were thirsty, invited strangers into your homes, clothed the needy, and visited the sick and the prisoners. When you did this for them, you were doing it for me."

The group to the right did these saving things unknowingly and will be really amazed with their very great reward.

So it will also be with the group on the left. They did not do these things, and Jesus as king and judge will command those pretenders on the left to the eternal path of punishment in fire for their unbelief, for not loving others, and for not doing any of those things done by those on the right. But the righteous ones will rejoice in eternal life in God's kingdom.

Ronald Chikonde (Matt. 26:1-14)
Passover and Anointing
When Jesus had finished a teaching, he told his disciples that the Passover feast was only two days away when the Son of Man would be handed over to be crucified. The elders of the temple were meeting together to find ways of arresting and killing Jesus in some tricky way. They assembled in the palace of the high priest whose name was Caiaphas. "But not during

the feast," they said, "or there will be a riot among the people."

Then, Jesus was in Bethany in the house of Simon who was once a leper. There came a woman with an alabaster jar of very expensive perfume, and she poured it on the head of Jesus as he was sitting at the table. The disciples saw this and were disappointed. "Why this waste?" they asked. "This perfume could have been sold at a very high price and the money used to help the poor."

Knowing their thoughts, Jesus told them, "Why are you worried with this woman? She has done a good thing to me. The poor you will always have to help, but you will not always have me. When she poured perfume on me, she did it to prepare for my burial." And Jesus told them that what the woman did would be remembered everywhere in the world where the gospel is taken. After that, one of the twelve—the one called Judas Iscariot—left to meet with the chief priest.

George Chikoya (Matt. 26:17-35)

The Lord's Supper

On the day of the unleavened bread feast, the Disciples asked Jesus where they should prepare the Passover meal. Jesus asked them to take this message to a certain man in the city: "The Teacher says his appointed time is near and wishes to celebrate Passover at your house." The disciples made the preparations, and as they ate the Passover meal Jesus said to them, "I tell you the truth, one of you will betray me."

This news made them most sad and they were saying, "Surely not I, Lord."

"Yes," Jesus said. "One who has dipped his hand into the bowl with me is going to betray me. It would be better for him if he had not been born."

"Surely not I, Rabbi," Judas said.

"Yes, it is you," Jesus said.

While they were eating, Jesus took the bread, gave thanks, broke it apart and said, "Take and eat, this is my body." Then he took the cup, gave thanks, and offered it to them saying, "Drink from it all of you. This is my blood of the covenant which is poured out for many for the forgiveness of sins. I tell you I will not drink anymore until I drink it new with you in my Father's kingdom."

They sang a hymn, then went out to the Mount of Olives where Jesus told them, "This very night you will all fall away on account of me for it is written, 'I will strike the Shepherd and the sheep will scatter.' But after suffering, I will go into Galilee."

Peter said, "Even if all fall away on account of you, I never will."

"The truth is," Jesus replied, "before the rooster crows you will deny me three times."

Peter insisted, "Even if I have to die with you, I will never disown you," and all the other disciples said the same.

Lemiter Kachinjika (Matt. 26:36-56)

Arrested

Jesus went to Gethsemane with his disciples and told them to sit while he went on ahead to pray. Along with him came the three close disciples, Peter and the two sons of Zebedee. In this moment Jesus was troubled with the terrible death that would soon happen to him.

Full of sorrow, Jesus told Peter and his companions to stay and keep watch with him. Then Jesus, with a broken heart, prayed earnestly: "My Father, if it is possible, may this cup be taken from me. Yet not what I want but what you want." After his prayer he went back to his disciples and found them sleeping. He was disappointed, but he encouraged them to keep watching and praying and overcoming temptation. Then he went to pray again and this time said, "My Father, if it is not possible for this cup to be taken away unless I drink it, may your will be done."

After Jesus finished his prayer, he went back to his disciples and found them sleeping a second time. He left them and went to pray for the third time—the same prayers as before. When he went back to the disciples he asked, "Are you resting well? But it is time to get up. It is time for me to be betrayed because my betrayer is coming here."

While Jesus was still speaking, along came Judas with a large crowd armed with swords and clubs. They were sent by the high priest and elders, and Judas betrayed Jesus with a kiss.

Then Jesus allowed those who came to fulfill their mission. As they were arresting Jesus, one of the disciples chopped off the ear of the high priest's servant, but Jesus told them not to fight and to put the sword away. A large army of angels could rescue him if that was needed. Rather, he explained, "This has taken place because all the writings of the prophets must come true."

Then all his disciples ran away.

George Lupande (Matt. 26:57-68)

The Sanhedrin

They took Jesus to the group of Jewish teachers and elders called the Sanhedrin where Caiaphas the high priest was all ready to hear the case. Peter followed at a distance and waited in the courtyard with the guards.

These leaders were looking for false evidence against Jesus so they could have an excuse to kill him, but the witnesses could not agree or find any reason for putting him to death. Then two men said, "This fellow said he can destroy the Temple of God and rebuild it in three days."

"What is your answer?" the high priest asked, but Jesus remained silent. In the questioning that followed they asked if indeed he was the Christ, the Son of God.

"Yes, it is as you say," Jesus replied. "In the future you will see the Son of Man sitting at the right hand of the Mighty One and coming on the clouds of heaven."

"Blasphemy!" said the high priest, tearing his clothes and saying, "Who needs more witnesses? You have heard him yourself. What do you think?"

"He is worthy of death," they all answered. They started to torture him, spitting in his face, striking him with their fists, slapping him and commanding him to prophesy about who hit him. But our Lord Jesus remained silent like a lamb ready to be sacrificed.

Danny Munkondia (Matt. 27:11-31)

Pilate

Jesus stood before the governor and they asked him, "Are you the king of the Jews?"

"Yes," he said. "It is as you say."

He was accused by the chief priest and elders but did not answer them. Pilate said, "Don't you hear the testimony they say about you?" But Jesus kept quiet.

Pilate's wife said to him, "Don't do anything to that innocent man, for I have suffered a lot today because of him."

Well, a government custom at the feast was to release one prisoner. So Pilate asked the crowd which prisoner to release, that notorious man called Barabbas, or Jesus?

The crowd said, "Barabbas!"

"Then what should I do with Jesus who is called Christ?" Pilate asked.

"Crucify him!" they shouted.

Pilate washed his hands with water in front of the angry mob and said, "I am innocent of this man's blood. He is your responsibility."

And all the people said, "Let his blood be on us and on our children."

So Pilate let Barabbas go free, but Jesus he had severely whipped and handed over to be crucified. Soldiers took Jesus into their official government building where they gathered around him, stripped him, put a scarlet robe on him, and twisted together thorns to put on his head.

Then they made fun of him by saying, "Hail, king of the Jews!" They spit on him and took the staff and struck him on the head again and again. After that they took off the robe and put his own clothes on him, and they led him away to crucify him.

Section 5 C: Expected One—
Suffering Servant

A story from the mother of MacDonald Chikankheni

A One-Eyed Mum

"I became one eyed because of you, my son." The mother who said this was just living somewhere in the village. In this family they had only one child whom they loved so much. Unfortunately, when the child was two years old his father passed away and he was left only with a mother. In the year of the death of his father, the child fell down and got injured up to the point that one eye was completely damaged. It was not functioning anymore.

His mother rushed to the doctors to see if they could assist in some way, but the doctor said, "This son will never see again with both eyes unless we remove that one damaged and replace it with one from someone else. If you can sacrifice your eye, mother, for the sake of your son, then we are ready to do the work."

The mother of this child accepted that idea and the doctors operated on both of them. The work they did was a success for the child started to see well with both of his eyes and left his mum one-eyed.

Then the son grew, his mum paid his school fees, and after school he got employed and married and his life completely changed for the better. But one thing with this man was that he was not feeling comfortable with his one-eyed mum—right up to the extent of wishing her to die.

One day his mum visited him at the town where he was living following his transfer. Having seen that his mother was coming from the distance, he rushed to her and gave her money for transport back home. He shouted, "I don't want to see you at my house you one-eyed woman! Here is the transport fee. Go back before people make me ashamed because of you. Crazy woman! Go!"

A year after this, his uncle came with a message that his mother was seriously ill, and the uncle forced him to come back to the village so the mother could see her son one last time. Having seen her son, the mother spoke her last words to him saying, "My son, forgive me for I have been a burden in your life. You have been despising me but still I love you. It is my time to go, but know this: I became one eyed because of my love for you, my son." Then his mum died.

The son wept for his mum and became senseless among all the people. Perhaps by now he was beginning to learn this wisdom: surely we should honor our parents.

McPherson Banda (John 19:5, 13-17)
Jesus Takes Up the Cross

When Pilate surrendered Jesus to the people, he said, "Here is the man." That time Jesus was in his crown of thorns. He was then brought out and Pilate sat down in the seat of judges at a place known as the stone pavement.

All this happened about the sixth hour during the preparations for the Passover. Pilate surrendered Jesus to the Jews, calling him their king, which made the Jews most angry and they shouted for him to crucify Jesus. "We have no king other than Caesar," they said.

Failing to defend Jesus, Pilate finally handed him over to them for crucifixion. Soldiers made him carry his own cross on the way to the killing place known as Golgotha.

Nelson Banda (John 1:29)

Lamb of God

Thinking back, one can remember what John the Baptist said out there by the Jordan River. He saw Jesus coming and said, "Look! There is the Lamb of God! He takes away the sin of the whole world. He is the man who comes after me even though he was before me."

Blessings Chagomerana (Luke 2:25-40; John 19:26-27)

Mother Mary

The Law of Moses said the oldest boy in a family belongs to the Lord, so at the right time Joseph and Mary took the baby Jesus to Jerusalem to present him to God. Now a righteous and devout man in Jerusalem named Simeon was waiting for Messiah to come. The Holy Spirit told him he would not die before seeing the Lord's Christ. Seeing little Jesus in the temple courts, Simon took him up and said to God, "Sovereign Lord, you have met your promise; now I can die peacefully, for my eyes see your salvation—light for Gentiles and glory for Israel."

Simon blessed them and said to Mary, "Many will rise and fall because of him. The thoughts of many hearts will be exposed, and a sword will pierce your soul."

Also at the temple was a very old woman prophet named Anna. She always fasted and prayed at the temple, and today she was there too. She gave thanks to God for Jesus and talked about him to anyone hoping for the Messiah. So after Joseph and Mary had done all the things required by God's law, they returned to Nazareth. Jesus grew up there to become strong, full of wisdom, and with the grace of God on him.

The mother of Jesus still lived to attend his crucifixion. As she watched him die he said to her, "Dear woman, here is your son," and to the disciple he loved who was standing there he said, "Here is your mother." So that disciple took care of her from that time on.

MacDonald Chikankheni (Mark 15:21; 8:34; 2 Tim. 2:3)
Simon Carries the Cross
My wife: Darling, on my way to market to buy fish I met
>   our neighbor's wife, and as you know, they are
>   Muslims. She asked me about my faith in Jesus, and
>   when I answered her that Jesus is my Lord and
>   precious Savior by saying that he died for my sin,
>   she totally disagreed with that. She said Jesus fled
>   away when he gave that cross to a man on his way

to Golgotha. So I had difficulty defending the death of Jesus. How can you help me?

Me: You know what, Madam? You as the wife of a pastor must know very well about the stories of the Bible—especially about our savior Jesus.

My wife: But you know dear, that most of my time I am busy here doing many things being a housewife, so it's hard for me to learn many stories fast and easy.

Me: Oh, don't worry. I will tell you the story of that man. His name is Simon from Cyrene.

My wife: Please tell me the story.

Me: So, when Jesus was on his way to Golgotha which means "the place of the skull," the heavy cross on his shoulder tired and exhausted him. Then they met the man Simon who was maybe on his journey to Jerusalem to attend Passover. The Roman soldiers forced him to carry the cross for Jesus, not for himself, and the soldiers were there all the way until Golgotha, and it was Jesus crucified on that cross.

My wife: So should we say that Jesus' words were fulfilled when somewhere he said, "Those who want to come after me must deny themself, take up their cross every day, and follow me"?

Me: For sure. You see, Simon did that in the actual way of picking up the real cross, but I believe that verse has a deeper meaning. It tells us to persevere through any hardship and put God's will first in our daily living.

My wife: Darling, I now know the story about this man Simon who helped Jesus carry the cross.

Me: Yes, and even the Apostle Paul in that second letter to Timothy wrote about the same thing, that we should endure hardship, persecutions, famine, and anything else—just like the farmer who works hard with the hope that one day he will see a harvest. Therefore, let's not give up.

My wife: Indeed, Jesus died for all including we Africans. So then, I see this way of the cross is most important. I will tell this true story about Simon from the Bible to my neighbor at market tomorrow.

Ronald Chikonde (Isa. 53:2-3; Matt. 25:40)

The Humble One

The Prophet Isaiah said this about the Messiah: he grew up like a tender young plant, coming in a humble way and growing up through a difficult childhood—like a root in dry ground. This Messiah had nothing beautiful about his physical appearance, and people considered him a mere man.

Looking at him as an ordinary man, they despised him. They did not accept him. But the mission of his coming was in his heart, and this was a mission of sorrow and suffering. He was not loved by people—they turned their faces away from him, they looked down on him, they failed to respect him.

And to those who treated people in that way, the king will answer, "Anything you have done to these ordinary, least important brothers of mine, you have done to me."

George Chikoya (Psalm 38:6-22)
Jesus Stumbles

All day long I am brought down very low. My back is filled with searing pain. There is no health in my body, and I am feeble and crushed. My anguished heart groans. My heart pounds; my strength fails. Light has left my eyes and because of my wounds my friends have left my side. Those who want to kill me set traps and think all day long about how to bring me to ruin.

I am like a dead man who can't hear; like a mute who can't speak. I am about to fall. Pain is always with me. All my good is being repaid with evil. O Lord, do not forsake me. O my God, come quickly to help me.

Lemiter Kachinjika (Luke 23:27-31; Matt. 7:21)

Jesus Consoles Women

When Jesus was on the way to Mount Calvary, a large group of people followed him, including women who mourned and wailed. When Jesus heard them, he turned to them and said, "Daughters of Jerusalem, do not weep for me. Weep for yourselves and your children." And he warned them about the terrible suffering that will take place later.

On those days of suffering, people will ask mountains to crush them and hills to cover them so they may die because of the painful suffering they will experience. Jesus finished by saying, "If men do these things when the tree is green, what will happen when it is dry?"

Not everyone who says to him "Lord, Lord," will enter the kingdom of heaven, but only the one who does the will of the Father who is in heaven.

George Lupande (Ps. 37:23-24; Heb. 4:15-16)

A Hard Way to Walk

The person in whom the Lord delights is the one who follows God, trusts him, and tries to do his will though it is a hard way to walk. It is full of stumbling blocks, but God will not let such a person fall. God will make his steps firm and will hold him up with a mighty hand.

Now we have a high priest who can sympathize with our weakness because Jesus was tempted in every way that we are, but he was without sin. Knowing that Jesus faced temptations, he is worthy to sympathize with us. We can be encouraged. We are to approach God with prayers. We are to come to him with confidence. He is there to put his peace and grace on us and help us in the true time of need.

No matter how difficult the way, he can help us through because he once passed the same way. As he fell when carrying the cross, so he understands our stumbling—and how to rise up again. So he is able to help us.

Danny Munkondia (John 19:23-24; Ps. 22:16-18)

Jesus Stripped of Garments

The soldiers who crucified Jesus divided his clothes into four shares, one for each of them—but not the undergarment. This item had no seams but was woven in one piece from top to bottom.

"Don't tear that," they said, "Let's decide by chance which one of us will get it." Doing this fulfilled the scripture which promised, "They divided my garments among them and cast lots for my clothing."

A Psalm of David predicted these happenings:

I am surrounded by dogs,

Circled by a band of evil men.

May hands and feet they have pierced,

I can count all my bones.

People stare at me and gloat,

Dividing my garments among them.

For my clothing they cast lots.

Chifundo Patrick (Luke 23:33-43; John 19:1)

Jesus Nailed

Pilate took Jesus and had him severely whipped in public, then the chief priests, the rulers, and the people led him away to be nailed on a wooden cross at a place called the Skull. Two criminals were also condemned to be nailed on crosses until they were dead, one on each side of Jesus.

After they crucified him, Jesus said to the Father, "Father, forgive them, for they do not know what they are doing." Then those who nailed him divided up his clothes by casting lots. Some people who stood there watching said, "He saved others—now let him save himself if he is Christ of God, the Chosen One."

The soldiers mocked him also, offering him wine vinegar and saying, "If you are the Jewish King, save yourself." There was a written notice above him that read, "This is the King of the Jews."

The criminal man nailed up on his left hand side said to Jesus, "Are you Christ? Then save yourself—and us!" But on his right hand side was the other crucified man who said, "Do you not fear God? We are under sentence as punishment for crimes we did. We are just getting what our deeds deserve. But this man has done nothing wrong." Then this law breaker said, "Remember me when you come into your kingdom."

Jesus said to him, "I tell you the truth, you will be with me in paradise today."

Hawa Phiri (John 19:28-37; Matt. 27:50)

Jesus Dies

Later, Jesus knowing he had completed everything and fulfilled every scripture about him, said, "I am thirsty." So they put a sponge soaked in wine vinegar on a stalk and held it up to his lips. Jesus received this drink and cried out loudly, "It is finished." With that Jesus gave up his spirit.

This was a special day of preparation for the Passover Sabbath and the Jews did not want dead bodies left on crosses for that celebration. So they asked Pilate to break the legs of the nailed-up ones to help them die, and then to take them down out of sight.

The soldiers did break the legs of the two men crucified with Jesus, but Jesus was already dead, so they did not break his legs. Instead, one soldier took a spear and pierced his side. Blood and water gushed out.

The man who saw this happen knows he is telling the truth and gives this report so you will also believe. When these things happened, they fulfilled the scripture that promised, "Not one of his bones will be broken," and "They will look on the one they have pierced."

P. Alufasi Phiri (John 19:38-40; Ps. 22:14-15)

Jesus Buried

Joseph of Arimathea wanted to see that Jesus was given a proper burial, but he wanted to do it secretly because he was afraid of the Jews. With Pilate's permission, he came and took the body away, accompanied by Nicodemus, a man who earlier had secretly visited Jesus at night. Nicodemus brought a mixture of myrrh and aloes, about 75 pounds of it. The two of them wrapped the body of Jesus with the spices into the strips of linen in accordance with standard Jewish burial customs.

The blood of Jesus was poured out like water and all his bones were out of joint. His heart became like wax and melted away within him. His strength dried up like a potsherd, and his tongue stuck to the roof of his mouth. He was laid into the dust of death.

Then Joseph placed Jesus in his own new tomb cut out of rock. He rolled a stone against the entrance, and Mary Magdalene and the other Mary were sitting there opposite the tomb and saw where the body was buried.

Billiat William (Matt. 28:1-15)

Jesus Rises from the Dead

Mary Magdalene and the other Mary went to look at the tomb of Jesus in the morning the day after the Sabbath. There was a big earthquake, and down from heaven came the Lord's angel who removed the stone door of the tomb and sat on it. The guards there were so afraid they shook and became almost dead.

"Do not be afraid," the angel said to the women. "I know you are looking for Jesus who was crucified. He is not here. He has risen as he said. Come, look at the place where he was. Then go quickly and tell his disciples he rose from death and goes ahead of you to Galilee. Go see him there. Now I have told you."

Full of joy, the women ran to tell the disciples when Jesus met them. "Hello," he said.

They reached for his feet and worshipped him there. "Don't be afraid," he told them. "Go tell my brothers to meet me in Galilee."

Some of those tomb guards went to the priests to tell what happened. They received a lot of money and were taught to say—if anyone asked what happened—that followers of Jesus came and stole the body while they were sleeping. This fable of theirs continues to be told among some Jews.

Chifundo Patrick (Luke 24:13-35)

Road to Emmaus

Two men were going to a village called Emmaus. It was seven miles from Jerusalem. These two men were discussing with one another about Jesus Christ and what had happened in the days past. As they talked, Jesus himself came up and walked along with them. They were kept from recognizing him, and he asked what they were talking over.

Those men stood still, their faces downcast. But one of them—his name was Cleopas—said, "Are you the only visitor to Jerusalem who does not know what happened there these past days?"

"What things?" Jesus asked.

"About Jesus of Nazareth," he said. "He was a prophet, powerful in word and deed before God and all the people. Yet the chief priests and our rulers handed him over to be sentenced to death by crucifixion. And what is more, now is the third day since all this took place. But some of our women amazed us. They went to the tomb early this morning, but they did not find his body. They came and told us they had seen an angel who said he was alive! Our companions went to the tomb and also found nothing—just as the women had said."

"How foolish you are," Jesus spoke, "how slow of heart to believe all that the prophets have said! Did not the Christ have to suffer those things and then enter his glory?" Then Jesus explained to them all that was said in the scriptures by the prophets about himself.

As they approached the village, Jesus seemed intent on going further, but they urged him strongly saying, "Please stay with us. It is nearly evening. The day is almost over."

So he stayed a while with them, and when he was at the table with them he broke bread, gave thanks, and gave it to them. Then their eyes were opened and they recognized him—but just then he disappeared!

They got right up and hurried back to Jerusalem where they found the eleven disciples and those with them rejoicing because they also knew the Lord was risen. "He appeared to Simon!" they said. Then the two from Emmaus told everything that happened to them, and how Jesus was recognized by them when he broke the bread.

Hawa Phiri (John 20:19-31)
Jesus, Disciples, Thomas
On the evening of the first day of the week, when the disciples were together with doors locked in fear of

Jews, Jesus appeared to them. He said, "Peace be with you," and he showed to them his hands and side. Seeing he was raised from the dead, the disciples were very happy and spilling with joy. He also said to them, "As the father has sent me, I am sending you. Receive the Holy Spirit. If you forgive anyone his sins, they are forgiven, and if you do not forgive them, they are not forgiven."

The disciple Thomas was not there, so he would not believe the others who said they had seen Jesus. "Unless I can put my finger into the nail marks in his hands and put my hand into his side," Thomas said, "I will not believe you."

A week later the disciples were in the house again and Thomas was with them. The door was locked, yet Jesus came and stood among them. Again he said, "Peace be with you." Then he said to Thomas, "Come! Put your finger here in my hands. Reach out and put your hand into my side. Stop doubting and believe."

Thomas said to him, "My Lord and my God!"

Jesus said to him, "Because you have seen me, you believe. Blessed are those who have not seen and yet believe."

Jesus did many more miraculous things than have been written down. But these are written that you may believe that Jesus is the Christ, the Son of God.

P. Alufasi Phiri (Matt. 28:16-20; Mark 16:19-20)

Great Commission and Ascension

Eleven remaining disciples of Jesus went to Galilee to the mountain where Jesus had told them to meet him. When the disciples saw him, they worshiped him, but some of them were in doubt.

Then Jesus came to meet with them and said, "All authority in heaven and on earth has been given to me. Therefore go and make disciples for all nations. Baptize them in the name of the Father and of the Son and of the Holy Spirit. Teach them to obey everything I have commanded you. And surely I am with you always to the very end of the age."

After Jesus spoke these words to them, he was taken up into heaven and sat at the right hand of God. Then the disciples went out and preached everywhere. The Lord worked with them and showed the word they spoke was true by putting miracles with the words.

Winiko Wanyetha (Isaiah 53:1-12)

The Arm of the Lord

Who believes our message?
Who has seen the Lord's mighty arm?
He grew up like a tender shoot,
Like a root of the dry ground.
He held for us no attraction;
Nothing desirable in his appearance.
Men despised and rejected him,
One who knew sorrows and suffering.
We ignored him;
We looked the other way.

For sure, he took our sickness
And carried our sorrows.
We thought God had struck him,
Smitten him, and afflicted him.
But he was pierced for our sins;
Crushed for our evil thoughts and actions.
Punishments that brought us peace
Were put on him.
By his wounds, we are healed.
Like sheep, we have all gone astray,
Each of us lost in our own way.
And the Lord loaded him down

With all of our iniquities.

Oppressed and afflicted,
Yet he said not a word.
Silent like a lamb to the slaughter,
Like a sheep being sheared,
He did not open his mouth.
He was taken away
By oppression and judgment.
Who can speak of his descendants?
He was cut off from the living
Stricken for our transgression,
Assigned a grave with the wicked,
With the rich in his death.
Yet he had done no violence,
He had spoken no deceit.

It was the Lord's will to crush him,
To cause him to suffer,
To make his life a guilt offering.
Yet he will see his offspring!
He will prolong his days!
The will of the Lord
Will prosper in his hand!
And after the suffering of his soul

He will see the light of life!
He will be satisfied!

By his knowledge my righteous servant
Will justify many.
He will bear their iniquities.
Therefore I give him a portion among the great.
He will divide the spoils with the strong
Because he poured out his life
And was numbered with transgressors.
Yes! He bore the sins of many and made
Interecession for transgressors.

Billiat William (John 1:1-18)

The Word

In the beginning there was the Word. This Word was with God and was God who spoke all things into being. That Word was the life and light of men. The light shines in dark places but the darkness does not understand.

One day a man named John was sent by God to tell about the true light that gives light to every person in the world. He was on the earth, and through him the world was made, yet the people of the world did not recognize him. He came to his own, but they did not receive him.

Yet to all who do receive him—those who believe his name—those ones he makes into children of God.

The Word became flesh and lived here with us, and we have seen his glory. This One came from the Father, full of grace and truth. John reported about him saying, "This is the One who comes after me even though he was before me." We all receive one blessing after another because of his grace. Moses gave us the law; Jesus gives us grace and truth.

Section 6: God's People Today

A story from the grandfather of Ronald Chinkonde:

Matola Tola (One Who Picks Up Anything)

Once upon a time in a certain village there lived a family of the name Bgamalala who had no children. They tried to seek help from herbalists and some doctors, but it never worked, so one day they heard news that a certain woman was doing a good job by the help of spirits.

They agreed to go there, and it worked—they were soon pregnant and the wife gave birth to a strange thing. This thing was just a human head of a boy without a body. When this family thought of the long journey to the spirit doctor and the money and time wasted, they were very sad. "I don't want to see it," Mr. Bgamalala said angrily.

But the wife said calmly, "My husband, let's keep this head and see what the Lord has given us. If it is a curse, let it be." So after a long time of conversation they agreed to keep the head.

The head grew up and when it reached the time to marry, his mother took the head in the basket and went around the village searching for a suitable girl for their son. But instead of being welcomed in many homes, they were insulted by girls who said they can't marry a head without a body—that was total madness! So the mother was very worried because she felt nothing but rejection.

When she decided to go back home she met the girl named Matola Tola. She is the one who picks up anything. Sure enough, the girl accepted the head. After accepting the head she was insulted and mocked by the people, but she said, "It's my choice, so please leave me alone. It's my life!" Even so, people kept on talking until they were tired.

The wife of the head was living with her in-laws with the younger brother of the head also living in her house. One day when the young brother was sleeping, at midnight as he woke up to pass urine, he was amazed to see a white man coming from the bedroom of his brother the head. As he reached the sitting room, the house was electrified and was full with chairs, fridges, tables, TV screens—everything was there! The boy was amazed and had a sleepless night, but before daybreak the white man went back again to his bedroom and everything in the house became as usual.

This happened for a long time and finally the brother of the head told about this happening to his sister-in-law, but she was doubting what he told her. So he said, "This night I will tie a string around your leg and put the other end where I can pull on it to awaken you when the amazing thing happens again."

That night the amazing thing happened again. The boy pulled the string and his sister-in-law was awakened. She saw the white man and the electrified room and was filled with fear and disbelief. So they realized the white man was coming out of the head and they agreed to destroy the head at midnight after the white man came out. They said, "This night this thing is going to happen!"

So at midnight when it happened again, the woman destroyed the head. Before daybreak the white man went back to the bedroom only to find there was no head! He had to remain as he was! And everything in the electrified house also remained—chairs, fridges, tables, TV screens!

Then those people who were insulting and mocking Matola Tola began to admire her and say she was blessed to be married to this white man and to live in his electrified house. This story is teaching us that we should not judge by outward appearances because we never know what is inside.

Fred K. Bamus (Acts 1:1-11)

Jesus Returns to Heaven

This book of Acts mentions all the things Jesus did and taught up to the day he was lifted to heaven. He was showing himself to his disciples alive during 40 days, and teaching them the good news of the kingdom of God. He ordered them not to move from Jerusalem but wait for the promise of God that they will receive the Holy Spirit.

They asked Jesus if he would remake the kingdom of the Jews at that time, but Jesus told them it was not their responsibility to know the time and condition which God set for his own plan. But they would receive the power when the Holy Spirit came upon them and would become his witnesses in Jerusalem, Judea, and Samaria and to the very end of the world.

While they were still seeing with their eyes open, Jesus ascended to heaven and was received into the clouds from their faces. Then two men wearing white robes stood beside them and said they should not wonder because Jesus will return from heaven in the same way he was going up.

McPherson Banda (Acts 2:1-13)

Pentecost

The festival of Passover pointed to the time when the Lamb of God would be sacrificed on the cross to forever pay for our sins. Fifty days later came the festival of Pentecost marking the time when the Law of God was given to Moses, but at this special Pentecost the law of God would be fulfilled. It happened this way:

All the Jesus followers were together when noise like powerful wind from heaven filled up their house. They saw something like fire on each of them. Filled with the Holy Spirit, they began speaking in many languages. Some Jews who had come to celebrate Pentecost heard this noise and realized each of them was hearing a message in their own language—yet all the men speaking were from Galilee!

These visitors were Parthians, Medes, and Elamites. Others were from Mesopotamia, Judea, Cappadocia, Pontius, Asia, Phyrgia, Pamphylia, Egypt and Libya. Still others were Romans, Cretans, and Arabs—all of them heard the wonders of God in their own language! Most of these people were amazed but some thought the speakers were drunk, so Peter stood up and spoke to all of them. Here is what he said:

"We're not drunk—it's only nine o'clock in the morning! No, this is what Joel the prophet spoke about, that in the last days God will put his Spirit on all people—both boys and girls, men and women, old people and young. Also there will be wonders in both earth and sky: blood, fire, and smoke. The sun will turn dark and the moon red before the glory day of the Lord. And everyone will be saved who calls on the Lord.

Nelson Banda (Acts 2:14-41)

Peter's Sermon

Then Peter told them all about Jesus, the Messiah who was recently crucified but who rose from the dead because he was that one David spoke about: "You will not abandon me to the grave or let your Holy One see decay."

Peter said he and those with him were witnesses that God raised Jesus to life and put him in heaven at the right hand of God. "God made Jesus, who you crucified, both Lord and Christ," Peter said.

The people who heard this news felt as if their hearts were cut. "This is very bad," they said to Peter. "Now what should we do?"

"Repent of your sin and be baptized in the name of Jesus Christ to be forgiven. Then you also will receive the gift that is the Holy Spirit. The promise is for you, for your children, and for anyone who the Lord will call."

The listeners who accepted this message were baptized, and about 3,000 people joined the followers of Jesus on that day.

Blessings Chagomerana (Acts 2:42-47; Acts 4:32-5:11)

The Church Begins

When the church began, believers were well understanding and obeying the apostles' teachings. They prayed and fellowshipped together as they witnessed the miraculous signs done by the apostles. They loved one another and shared their possessions. No one lacked anything among them, for they sold their land and houses and other possessions and shared it with the believers in common or gave it to anyone who had a need.

They met every day in the temple and the Lord increased them in number daily. With the grace of God, the apostles continued to preach the gospel. One day Barnabas sold a field of his and brought the money to the church. But Ananias and his wife Sapphira sold a piece of property and secretly put back for themselves some of the money. When Ananias took the other money to the apostles, Peter saw a problem.

"Why do you let Satan deceive you?" he asked. "You have lied to the Holy Spirit! The land was yours and the money was yours also. Why did you do this bad thing?"

Immediately Ananias fell down and died. Then young men took him out and buried him. Later his wife came, knowing nothing of what happened to her husband. Peter asked her if they sold the land at that certain price, and she said that for sure, it was really the price.

So Peter said, "Why would you agree to test the Spirit of the Lord? Your husband is already dead and buried. You will die also," and immediately she died. The young men came and took her body out and buried her beside her husband. The church and those who heard about this became fearful at this true story.

MacDonald Chikankheni (Acts 5:17-41)

Persecution Begins

Then some religious leaders were not comfortable and they felt bad about those apostles who were teaching the gospel of Jesus, so they captured them and threw them in jail. But in the night, the angel of the Lord rescued the apostles and encouraged them to carry on with the work of spreading this life-giving good news of our Lord Jesus—and they did. They took the word everywhere.

While the religious leaders and court officials were holding a meeting, they sent a captain to bring the apostles in before them from the jail. They were all shocked to find that no one was in the jail except the soldiers who were guarding outside, and even the doors were still locked. At that time they had nothing to do. They were all empty headed.

Suddenly they got the news that the apostles were teaching right there in the temple. Taking immediate action, they sent soldiers to bring the apostles before the court, but peacefully, for they were afraid of people who would not agree with putting the apostles on trial.

In court the apostles were told to stop preaching the gospel about Jesus. But Peter and his friends told the court, "We must obey God." They said they would remain obedient to witnessing for God the Father, the Son, and the Holy Spirit, and never give up due to men's influence.

This response stirred up the murderous anger in the religious leaders and court officials toward the apostles, but this man called Gamaliel, the teacher of the law, stood in opposition to their anger. He reminded them of some men who were murdered for other work like this—and nothing came of their teachings. He also warned about an unsuccessful future for the Jewish leaders if they continued fighting these men if they were in fact serving God. So he said they better just let these men go.

This man's words cooled down their anger toward the apostles, but the court still ordered that they be beaten and then released. So the apostles were set free, rejoicing because of their sufferings for Christ, and they continued spreading the gospel daily everywhere.

Ronald Chikonde (Acts 8:1-8; 26-40)

Philip the Missionary

In those days great trouble broke out against the church at Jerusalem and all except the apostles were pushed beyond Jerusalem into Judea and Samaria. The gifted preacher Stephen was stoned to death. Godly men put to rest Stephen and mourned deeply for him, but that angry man Saul began to destroy the church, going into houses by force and taking men and women for prison.

Those who scattered preached the word wherever they went. Philip went to Samaria and preached about Christ. A huge number of people listened to Philip. They saw wonderful works and signs he did and paid close attention to what he said. Evil spirits made shouts and came out of many people. People who were lame or couldn't walk were healed, so there was much happiness in that city.

An angel of the Lord spoke to Philip: "Go south to the desert road," he said. That's the road going from Jerusalem to Gaza. So Philip went, and he met an important Ethiopian official, positioned in charge of all the riches of Candace the queen of Ethiopia. He had gone to Jerusalem to pray. On his way home he was reading the book of Isaiah the prophet while sitting in his chariot.

"Go close to that chariot," the Holy Spirit told Philip, so he ran up and heard the man reading.

"Do you understand that?" Philip asked.

"How can I?" he said. "I need someone to explain it to me," so he invited Philip to come up and sit with him. The part the official was reading says, "He was taken to be killed like a sheep. Just as lambs are silent while their wool is being cut off, he did not open his mouth—not even when he was treated badly and judged wrongly. Who can say anything about his children? His life was cut off from the earth."

The official said to Philip, "Tell me, please. Who is the prophet talking about? Himself, or someone else?"

So Philip began in that part of scripture and told him the good news about Jesus. As they went along the road they came to some water. "Look!" said the official, "Here is water! Why shouldn't I be baptized?" He commanded that the chariot should stop.

Philip and the official went into the water and Philip baptized him. When they came out of the water the Spirit of the Lord took Philip away. The official did not see him again but went on his journey joyfully. Philip was seen next at Azotus, and from there he traveled all around. He preached the good news in all the towns until finally he arrived in Caesarea.

George Chikoya (Acts 9:1-19)

Saul follows Jesus

Saul was still looking for the Lord's disciples to kill them. He went to the high priest to get permission documents. After he got those letters, he went on a journey to Damascus. As he drew near to that city, a light from heaven flashed onto him. He fell on the ground and heard a voice that said, "Saul, Saul, why are you persecuting me?

Saul asked the voice what it was. It responded, "I am Jesus, the one whom you're persecuting. Now get up and go to that city and over there I will tell you what to do.

Even the men there with Saul heard the voice noise but did not see what Saul did. They just took hold of the hands of Saul—because he was now blind—and went to Damascus where for three days he never ate or drank anything.

In Damascus the Lord spoke to Ananias in a vision. The message was to go to a particular house, find a man from Tarsus, and pray for him. Ananias told God this man Saul was a bad and dangerous person who wanted to hurt the church. God said not to worry, for this man will become a tool in God's hands to take the good news of Jesus to Gentiles.

Ananias did everything just as the Lord told him: He went and prayed for Saul. Then the Holy Spirit filled that evil man, something like scales of fish fell down from the eyes of Saul, he was no longer blind, and he was baptized. Then they ate food.

Lemiter Kachinjika (Acts 11:19-30)

The Antioch Church

Now those people who were scattered because of the great persecution in the days of Stephen, they reached to Phoenicia, Cyprus, and Antioch, preaching to Jews only. Some of them were men who came from Cyprus and Cyrene. They went to the Gentiles and preached the good news of our Lord Jesus Christ. God's hand was with them, and a big crowd of people believed and turned to the Lord.

This news reached Jerusalem and they sent Barnabas to Antioch. Barnabas saw the grace of God on them and was glad. He encouraged them to remain true to the Lord. He was a good man and full of the Holy Spirit, so a great number were brought to the Lord.

Then Barnabas went to Tarsus to find Saul, who they now called Paul, and took him along back to Antioch. They stayed there a whole year teaching in the big, new church. During those days a prophet named Agabus stood there in the power of the Holy Spirit to say a famine was coming, and this prophesy came true in the days of the Roman leader Claudius. So the people of Antioch sent help to their brothers who lived in Judea. Barnabas and Paul took the gift from the Antioch church to the elders of the church in Jerusalem.

George Lupande (Acts 13:1-12; Acts 14:21-28)

Missionaries Sent

The church of Antioch included some prophets and teachers—people like Barnabas, Simeon, and then Saul. When they were worshiping and having a fasting, the Holy Spirit told them to separate out Barnabas and Saul to the work of the Lord. They placed their hands on them and sent them off. So those new missionaries arrived at Salamis where they started proclaiming the word of God in Jewish synagogues.

In that town was a sorcerer called Bar-Jesus who was trying to make people not have faith in the word of God. Saul, having been filled with the Holy Spirit, told him that he was going to be blind for a time—and immediately he became blind. When the proconsul saw this miracle, he became a believer of God.

When they traveled to such towns as Lystra, Iconium, and Antioch, they preached the good news and more disciples were strengthened in their faith. The preachers promised the followers of Jesus that many hardships come with entering the kingdom of God, so they must be strong.

Saul (now called Paul) and Barnabas appointed church elders after prayers and fasting. Whenever they left a town, they turned over all the new believers to the grace of God. Finally, they returned to Antioch in Syria where they gathered all the people of the church and gave a report about what God did through them, saying God has opened the door for the Gentiles and they have come to faith. Then they stayed there for a long time.

Danny Munkondia (Rom. 1:18-32)

God's Wrath Explained

God's fierce anger is being made known from heaven against all the godlessness and wickedness of people who suppress the truth. Since the creation of the world God has been easy to understand by anyone. God's invisible character, eternal power, and divine nature can be clearly seen in everything that has been made.

Although they never glorified God or gave thanks to him, they knew him. Their minds became idle and their foolish hearts dark. They seemed to be intelligent but they were not. The glory of immortal God they traded for birds, animals, and mortal man, so God gave them over in the sinful desires they had for sexual impurity and degrading their bodies. They exchanged the truth of God for lies; they worshipped the creation instead of the Creator.

God gave up on them because they had shameful lusts. Women exchanged natural relations with men for unnatural relations with other women. Men abandoned natural relations with women and lusted for men. People did things not fit to be done, so God gave them up to corruption, doing what ought not to be done. Even though they knew God's righteous decrees, every kind of wickedness filled them.

Chifundo Patrick (Rom. 8:1-17)
The Spirit Brings Life

All those people who live in Christ Jesus are free! The law of the Spirit life sets them free from the law of death. The mind of the sinful is death, but the Sprit gives eternal life and peace. The mind of the sinful refuses God and does not submit to God, but God sent Himself in a human body to be a sin offering. Those who live by the sinful nature are just taking care for their body, but those who live by the Spirit are taking care of the spiritual.

The mind of the sinful is death, but those caring of the Spirit face eternal life and peace. The minds of sinful people are refusing God and do not submit to God, but those who live through the Spirit can please God.

Those who have not the Spirit also have not Christ Jesus. But those who are in Christ have the Spirit of Christ in them. If Christ lives in you, even when your body dies because of sin, the Spirit will bring you alive again because of righteousness. The Spirit who raised Jesus from the dead will give life again to our dead bodies through the Spirit.

We are the children of God. So we are not receiving the spirit of slavery or fear, but we are receiving the Spirit of sons who call God their daddy. The Spirit himself agrees with our spirit that we are children of God. But if we have received suffering, we share the inheritance of Christ, and we also share in his glory.

Hawa Phiri (Rom. 11:33-12:2)

Transformed Ones

Oh how deep are the riches of God!
How deep his wisdom and knowledge,
How complex his judgments.
His pathways cannot be traced
Unless you follow him most closely.

Who can know that great mind of His?
No human could ever give him advice,
Or even give him anything at all.
All things are from him
And through him and to him.
To him be glory forever!
Yes!

Because his mercy is so great
We must offer ourselves to him

As holy and pleasing, living sacrifices.
This is true spiritual worship.

No longer are we to bend to patterns of this world.
We must bend our minds to the ways of God.
Then we can test and agree with God's will:
His good, pleasing, perfect will.

P. Alufasi Phiri (1 Cor. 13:1-13)

Most Excellent Way

There is nothing to the people who have no love. Not even if they speak the languages of men and angels. Such talk is just like the noise of a gong or cymbal— empty. Even if they can predict the future or understand the secret knowledge of God or have enough faith to move mountains from one place to another, that's all nothing without love.

Without love, nothing is gained even by giving all possessions to the poor or leaving our own bodies in a fire!

Love does not bring envy. It does not boast or brag. It's not rude, self-seeking, or easily angered. It does not keep track of when it is sinned against. It takes no delight in evil but celebrates truth. It is patient and kind.

Love is steady against pressure, it protects, and it gives hope. Love is the only genuine way to the Lord because it never fails.

Prophecies will stop, tongues will be quiet, and knowledge will pass away. But love will last while the imperfect disappears. Among the three great things of faith, hope, and love, the greatest is love.

Winiko Wanyetha (Eph. 5:1-21)

Imitators of God

We need to imitate God just as our much-loved children imitate us. We need to walk in love and sacrifice ourselves as Jesus did for us. We need to hate all evil like sexual immorality or any kind of impurity and things of the devil. Instead, we need to be the holy people who do good things. All people who do the evil things are not in the kingdom of God. Neither are people who worship idols.

Do not allow someone to deceive you with useless words, because God becomes sad with disobedient people. At first you were in darkness, but now you walk in light because of Jesus Christ. We get fruit of light in goodness, righteousness, and truth. Do not love dark work, because there is no profit in that for you. Evil work is shameful. Wake up, sleepers! Rise from the dead and Christ will shine on you.

Be careful how you live, not as unwise but as wise people. My brother, do not be foolish, but proclaim what is God's will. Do not drink wine that leads to loss but be filled with the Holy Spirit. Speak to one another the psalms, hymns, and spiritual songs that praise God in your heart. All the time give thanks to God the Father for everything, in the name of our Lord Jesus Christ. Submit to one another out of reverence for Christ.

Billiat William (1 Tim. 2:1-6)

Prayer Instructions

Pray and give thanks for everyone—for presidents and dictators and anyone in authority. Such praying helps us live peacefully and quietly, practicing our godliness and holiness.

This kind of praying is good and pleases God who wants everyone to escape sin and know truth. The one go-between from man to God and back again is the man Jesus Christ who paid the death penalty for our sins—no one else has ever done that.

Section 7: In the New Beginning

A story from the father of George M. Chikoya:

The HIV Hyena

In our community, grandparents tell stories mostly about how the youth can behave well during the stage between puberty and adulthood, the ages of 14-25 for men and 12-21 for girls.

This is a serious stage. Boys and girls experience new development in their bodies and also sexual desires are high enough. So grandparents need to give boys and girls careful instructions on how they can develop skills for decision making and problem solving, and also how they can choose a good partner into marriage.

Stories are often told at night soon after dinner around the cooking fire while the moon is shining. Mostly these stories are held at grandparents' houses, and those who do not have grandparents try to join the nearby grandparents.

Important: The stories are mostly done by people of the same sex—female grandparent to girls and male grandparents to boys—for better understanding to each other. Here is one such story:

My father told me a story about some of the cultural practices and beliefs that caused the spread of HIV and AIDs in the early 1980s among the youth in our community. The youth have to go through initiation ceremonies—Chimanwali for girls and Circumcision for boys. This story is about initiation ceremonies for girls.

Girls within the ages from 10 to 13 were initiated by elderly women called Namkungwi (counselors). After the initiation process, the elderly identify an older man to have sex with all initiates to prove if they have mastered what they were taught at the Tsimba (the initiation hut).

This man is known as frsi (hyena) because he has to perform his duty only at night without revealing his identity. All the girls were forced to have sex with this man as it was required by the custom. Through this process the following things might happen:

- Frsi could be infected with HIV and therefore spread the infection to many girls at once since one initiation ceremony often involves 20 to 30 girls.
- It has also been observed that the girls who went for initiation have high sexual desire within the period after they come out from Simba.

- The girls are also told how to use love potions with their husbands as they get into marriage. So this may lead more men to be silent about their wives when their wives have been found out having sex with other partners apart from their husbands.

But now the situation is a little improved due to the influence of some nongovernmental institutions that have come to help us survive the AIDS crisis. This is a true story.

Dan Runyon (Isa. 64:1-9)

Rip Open the Heavens!

Oh God! I wish you would rip open the heavens and come down. I wish you would shake the mountains like fire burns brush, like fire makes water boil, so that your enemies would know you, and so all nations would tremble at your presence.

You have done this before. Do it again! Since the beginning of the world there has never been a God like you. You respond to the one who waits for you. You meet with the one who rejoices in doing right. You remember those who remember you.

But we are unclean. Our best efforts are like filthy rags. We fade away like dry leaves. We are blown away by the wind for our iniquities. None of us holds to you or asks for you. No wonder you hide from us and we are consumed by our sins.

But now! O Lord, you are our father. We are the clay; you are the clay worker. Mold us into your image; do not remember our sins forever. Look at us—we are your people!

Fred K. Bamus (1 Tim. 4:1-6; 2 Pet. 2:4-9)

Things Taught by Demons

The Spirit tells that in last days people will lose their faith and follow spirits which make people stray from the truth to believe things taught by demons. These false teachers are cheaters. Their minds are pierced by hot metal. They say people can't marry. They stop people from eating perfectly good food that God created for those who know the truth and are thankful for their food.

Everything God made is good; nothing should be wasted if people receive it with thanksgiving, for it becomes good with the word of God and prayer. If you warn the brothers of this deception, you will be a good minister, true to the faith, and good with the instructions you follow.

Think about this: God sent the angels who rebelled to hell, keeping them in deep holes of darkness until the time of judgment. God destroyed the world he made with a flood because of great evil, but saved only Noah and seven others. God burned the cities of Sodom and Gomorah to ashes to provide an example of what happens to sinners, but saved only Lot and his daughters.

So we see that God knows how to save godly people while at the same time holding the evil ones in punishment until the judgment day.

McPherson Banda (Jude 4-13)

Teachings of Godless Men

Jude knew that some people known to be condemned had secretly slipped in among the believers. They were godless men who changed the grace of their God into a license to be immoral and even to deny Jesus Christ as their only sovereign and Lord.

Jude reminded them that even though the Lord delivered his people out of Egypt, he later destroyed those who did not believe. And angels who did not keep their positions of authority but abandoned their own home—those God has kept in darkness and tied in everlasting chains until the great judgment day.

In a similar way, Sodom and Gomorah and the surrounding towns became sexually immoral and perverse. Their destruction serves as an example of those who will suffer the punishment of eternal fire. And those dreamers who pollute their own bodies, reject authority, and slander heavenly beings are also condemned. Even the archangel Michael when he disputed with the devil about the body of Moses did not slander him but just said, "The Lord rebuke you."

Yes, those men spoke abusively against whatever they did not understand. And what things they did understand by instinct like wild animals, those were the very things that destroyed them. Woe to all such men slipping into the church! They are blemishes on your love feasts, yet you are eating with them without the slightest qualm.

But these are shepherds who feed only themselves. They are clouds without rain, blown along by the wind. They are like autumn trees without fruit and uprooted—twice dead. They are like wild waves of the sea, like stars that wander from their course, for whom the blackest darkness has been reserved forever.

Nelson Banda (Matt. 24:3-14)

Watch Out!

When he was sitting on the Mount of Olives, Jesus explained things that would happen in the future. He warned us about false prophets. Jesus knew some people will come in the name of him and do miraculous signs and saying they are the returned Christ. Although this will happen, don't follow them because they will mislead you. Expect wars and rumors of wars, nation against nation, kingdom against kingdom, earthquakes, persecution, hunger, and death. All this is just the beginning of the end.

Followers of Jesus will be hated by all nations. Some will leave the faith and hate and betray each other. False prophets will fool many people. Wickedness will heat up and love will cool down. The one who stands against all this to the very end will be saved. Good news stories of the kingdom of Jesus will be told to all the families of the whole world; only after that will the end come.

Blessings Chagomerana (Rev. 13:1-10)

The Beast

I stood on the shore of the sea and saw the beast come out of the water. It had seven heads and ten horns.

On those horns were ten crowns, and on its head were evil names full of profanity. The beast was like a leopard with hyena feet and a lion mouth. The Dragon gave this beast his throne, power, and authority. One of its heads seemed to have died but the death wound was healed.

The whole earth admired and followed it. People worshiped this dragon because it gave power and authority to the beast. They also worshipped the beast and said there was no one like it. It could talk and spoke big things about itself and wicked things against God, the temple, and those who live in heaven. Three years and four months were given to it for doing these things. It was also given authority to make war against the saints and rule over people.

People whose names are taken out of the book of life because of their sins will worship these pretend gods. Only those belonging to the Lamb who was slain from the creation of the world will not worship this beast.

If you have ears, listen to this: The one going into captivity, will indeed go into captivity; the one due to be killed by a sword will in fact die that way. Patient endurance and faithfulness are needed for the saints.

MacDonald Chikankheni (Rev. 1:9-18)

Son of Man

When the Lord Jesus was about to ascend to heaven, he promised his followers to not let them alone until the end of this age. The following story shows how Christ continued his fellowship with the faithful follower John.

John was at the island of Patmos where he was left as punishment for his preaching about Jesus. In that lonely place, Jesus visited John in a vision and told him to write down everything he saw and heard in their conversations and to send these writings to the seven churches in Asia minor.

When John looked to where the voice was coming from, he saw seven lamp stands and Jesus stood among them. His appearance was amazing. He was shining like a sun with glory while holding seven shining objects in his right hand, and calling himself the author and finisher of everything. Not just that, but also Jesus explained to John his eternity and his victory over the power of death. Jesus showed himself to be the everlasting One.

Ronald Chikonde (Rev. 4:1-11)

Throne in Heaven

John saw a door left open into heaven and heard a voice saying, "come in here and I will show you things to happen in the future." At once he was in the spirit, and inside that door he saw a throne in heaven with someone sitting on it. That one sitting on the throne looked like precious stones called jasper and carnelian. A rainbow like an emerald went around the throne.

In a circle around the throne were 24 other thrones. Sitting on them were 24 elders dressed in white and with gold crowns on their heads. Out of the big throne came lightning flashes and thunder rumblings. Something that looked like a very clear sea of glass spread out in front of that throne.

In the center, around the throne, were four living creatures covered with eyes in front and back. The first was like a lion, the second like an ox, the third had a man's face, the fourth was like a winged eagle. All four creatures had six wings and eyes in all places—even under their wings. All day and all night they kept on saying "Holy, holy, holy is the Lord God Almighty who was, and is, and is to come."

As the creatures gave glory, honor, and thanks to the one on the throne who lives for ever and ever, the 24 elders fell down before him and worshipped him who lives for ever and ever. They put their crowns before the throne and said, "You are worthy, our Lord and God, to receive glory and honor and power, for you created all things, and by your will they were created and have their being."

George Chikoya (Rev. 5:1-14)

Lamb of God

John saw the following in his vision: At the right hand of the one sitting on the throne was a long paper with writing on both sides. Seven seals held it together. A mighty angel said, "Who is qualified to break open the seven seals, open it up, and translate the signs of the book?" There was no one who could do that—not in heaven; not on earth.

I cried enough about this, because there was no one who could open the book. Then I heard a voice say the Lion of Judah could do it.

This Lion was a Lamb! He stood up in the center of the throne encircled by the four living creatures and 24 elders. He had seven horns and seven eyes—the seven spirits of God that go out into all the earth.

When he took the book from the right hand of the one on the throne, the creatures around him fell to the ground. In their hands were harps and gold bowls full of prayers from saints. Then they sang a song with these words:

> You are worthy to take the book
>
> And you are worthy to open the book.
>
> Your blood has bought people of every kind,
>
> From every family and language and land.
>
> You have made of them a kingdom
>
> To serve our God as priests
>
> And they will rule the earth.

Then John heard the voices of a 100 million angels circling the throne and singing very, very powerfully:

> The Lamb is worthy
>
> For he was killed.
>
> Now with power
>
> And wealth he's filled.
>
> Wisdom and strength are his,
>
> And honor, glory and praise.

Then John heard every creature God ever made—in heaven, earth, and sea—singing:

> Praise and honor and glory and power
>
> We give to him for ever and ever
>
> To the One sitting on the throne
>
> And to the Lamb, the holy One.

So shall it ever be, the living creatures said. And the elders fell down and worshipped Him.

Lemiter Kachinjika (Rev. 7:9-17)
Multitudes in Heaven

After this I saw a great gathering of people, so many no one could count them. These humans came from all nations and languages to stand before the throne in front of the Lamb. All of them were wearing white clothes and held palm branches in their hands.

Then the angels standing around the throne and the elders and the four creatures all bowed down their faces before the throne and worshipped God and said, "Amen! Praise and glory and wisdom and thanks and honor and power and strength shall be to our God ever and ever, amen!"

One of the elders asked me, "Who are these people wearing white clothes and where do they come from?"

Then I said to him, "My lord, you know yourself."

Then he said to me, "They came out from the great persecution and washed their clothes with the blood of the Lamb. That is why they serve him day and night in his temple. He who sits on the throne is their shelter. They will never be hungry and never be thirsty again.

The sun will not beat on them and they will not sweat, because the Lamb will shepherd them and lead them to springs of life. And God will wipe away all their tears."

George Lupande (Rev. 11:15-19)
Kingdom of our Lord

When the seventh angel sounded his trumpet, a loud voice in heaven said, "God has taken the kingdom of the world and with Christ they will rule it forever and ever."

Then the 24 elders who sat on the thrones before God fell on their faces and worshiped God by saying, "We thank you, God, the one who is and who was. You have all great power to rule the world. The time has come that you should judge the dead. And the time has come to reward your servants, prophets, and the saints, even those who feared your name, both children and adults."

After that, the temple of God opened and within the temple there was the ark of the covenant. When the door of God's temple opened, there were flashes of lightning, rumblings, thunders, and an earthquake. There was also a great hailstorm.

Danny Munkondia (Rev. 14:6-13)

Three Angels

Another angel came flying in midair. He had the gospel to declare publicly to those who are on earth and to every nation and tribe. He shouted and said, "Fear God and give glory since the time of judgment is here now. Worship him who made the heavens and earth, the sea and all rivers."

Another angel followed and said, "Humbled to the ground is Babylon the Great. She is fallen since she made all races of people drink the wine of her adulteries."

A third angel followed them and said in a big voice, "If someone pays divine honor to the beast and his images, he will get his mark on the forehead. He also will drink the wine of God's great anger which has been poured full strength into the cup of his fierce anger. He will be burned with burning sulfur in the presence of the holy angel. The smoke of their torment rises for ever and ever. Day and night there will be no rest for those who give honor to the beast and his image, for anyone who gets the mark of his name." This means patient suffering is necessary for saints who obey God and stay faithful to Jesus.

Then the voice from heaven said, "Blessed are the dead who die in the Lord from now on."

"Yes," the Spirit said. "They will get to rest from their labor, and all the fruit of their work will follow them."

Chifundo Patrick (Rev. 19:1-10)

Hallelujah

After those things I heard a deep loudness in heaven. It burst out like a huge crowd shouting, "Hallelujah!
Salvation, glory, and power belong to our God. The way he judges is true and fair. He has judged the great prostitute. She polluted the earth with her terrible sins. God has paid her back for killing those who served him."

Again they shouted, "Hallelujah!" The smoke from her fire goes up for ever and ever. The 24 elders and the four living creatures bowed down and worshiped God. They cried out, "Amen! Hallelujah! And praise God!"

Noise of the huge crowd came at me like the roar of rushing waters, like loud thunder shouting, "Hallelujah! Our Lord God is the King who rules over all. Let us be joyous and glad and give glory to him."

It was the time of the lamb's wedding. Fine linen, bright and clean, was given for the bride to wear. The fine linen stands for the right things that God's people do and the angel said to me to write this: "Blessed are those who are invited to the wedding supper of the lamb."

These are true words of God. I fell down to worship him but he said to me, "No! Do not worship me. I am a slave with you and your brothers to serve God just as you do. Worship God! For the witness of Jesus is the spirit of prophecy."

Hawa Phiri (Rev. 21 1-8)

New Heaven and Earth

God has promised the new heaven and the new earth to those who are believing him, to those with pure hearts, to those who trust him and have faith in Jesus Christ. When John was looking into heaven, he saw the new heaven and new earth—a world with no sea. And the new city Jerusalem comes out from God like a wife. She is prepared for her husband draped in cloth. This wife was the people of God, and God was with them, and they were with God. And God will wipe every tear from their eyes.

In that new earth there will be no more death, or mourning, or crying, or pain. All old things will have passed away and he will make everything new. For sure, because his words are trustworthy and true, and he is Alpha and Omega, Beginning and End. And those who are thirsty come to him and he gives them the water of life without paying anything; this is free water.

For the one who overcomes, he will be his God and he will be his son. But those who are fearful, cowardly, unbelieving, the vile, the murderers, the sexually immoral, all those who practice evil arts, idolators, and liars—for all these people there will be a place in the fiery lake of burning sulfur. This is the second death.

P. Alufasi Phiri (Rev. 21:9-12; 22-27)

New Jerusalem

There was one angel who came and talked to John at the island of Patmos. This angel was one of the seven angels who had the seven bowls full of the seven last plagues. The angel showed John the bride, the wife of the lamb. He also carried him away in the spirit to the very great and high mountain and showed him a holy city, which is the new Jerusalem coming down out of heaven from God. The city shone with the glory of God and it was very bright, like a very precious jewel, like jasper, clear as crystal. The city had a great high wall with twelve gates and names were written on the gates.

These were the names of the twelve tribes. The great street of the city was pure and gold like transparent glass.

The Lord God Almighty and the Lamb are in the city and God's glory brings the shine on it, and light on it, and like a lamp is the Lamb. And all nations will walk by its light, and all kings of earth will bring their splendor to it. The gate will be always open for there will be no night. Nations will bring their honor and glory into it. All who have their names written in the Lamb's book of life enter into it—but not the impure or anyone who does shameful or deceitful things to others.

Winiko Wanyetha (Rev. 22:1-6)

River of Life

John saw the clear water of a living river sparkling clean like a crystal. It came from God's throne and down a great street of the town. The tree of life stood on every side of the river having twelve crops of fruit. It gave fruit every month and its leaves could heal all nations.

There was no longer any curse on the land. The throne of God and the Lamb are in the city and his servants serve him. There will not be night and they will not need lights or even the sun, for the Lord our God will light this earth and be king there for ever and ever.

Then God said to John, "What I have said is faithful and true. God has sent his angel to show you things that will happen soon."

Billiat William (Rev. 22:10-17)

I Am Coming Soon

The time for these things to happen is near—the son of man is coming any moment. Meanwhile, those who are doing bad things will keep on in their badness, and those who are doing the good and right things will keep on in their ways. Those who are holy in Christ, let them keep on being holy to all.

"I am coming soon," Jesus told John. "I will have rewards to give everyone based on what he has done. I am Alpha and Omega, Beginning and End, First and Last. Blessed are those who are clean in their hearts. They will receive the right to eat the fruit from the tree of life and enter the gates of the city.

"In this world are those dogs, those who do magic, those sexually loose ones, those murderers, idol worshipers, and people who love falseness and lying. But I sent my angel to witness to the believers that I am both the Root of David's ancestry and also his Offspring—I am the shining star of the morning."

So this is the invitation: "Come!" The Spirit and the Bride say "Come! Come, anyone who wishes! Come, anyone who is thirsty! Come and have the free gift of the water of life."

The End

Tribal Bible Origins

Ryan and Jen Willson of the Great Commission Bible School in Lilongwe, Malawi, invited me to teach a world missions course for African pastors in training. They urged me to abandon Western styles of teaching and instead to respect and embrace the oral traditions of Africa. They recommended material at www.storyrunners.com to learn more appropriate teaching methods.

I also read Christine Dillon's *Telling the Gospel Through Story* (Downers Grove, IL: InterVarsity, 2012) for additional guidance. Nicholas Carr's *The Shallows* (New York: W.W. Norton, 2011) deepened my understanding of the ways in which oral tradition brain-function differs from those influenced by intellectual technologies deriving from the printed word. And Vishal Mangalwadi's *The Book that Made Your World* (Nashville: Thomas Nelson, 2011) gave me a deep appreciation for how the Bible created the soul of Western civilization.

Drastic changes to my teaching methods resulted from reading these books as I worked to capture the flavor of African oral tradition. What fun we had as my 15 students told Bible stories in their tribal languages, then labored to write them down and back-translate them to English (see samples on pages 195-197). Their stories give a strong taste of the gospel the way Jesus first told it—through stories often told to just a few folks gathered in villages.

My class selected Bible stories to capture the entire scope of the biblical narrative. The seven-act biblical drama outlined in the table of contents derives from *Introducing World Missions* by Scott Moreau, Gary Corwin, and Gary McGee (Grand Rapids: Baker Academic, 2004).

Discernment on how to tell the stories came from my niece Andrea, a Bible translator who provided the questions below. The answers of my students are summarized in parenthesis with the questions.

- *What do my people tell stories about?* (The history of our tribe, the places where our ancestors traveled, the wars they fought, and stories that instruct our young people on how to behave.)
- *Who tells stories?* (Mostly the grandfathers!)
- *What makes good stories?* (When they are accompanied by songs and dance, and when objects such as beans or maize or pieces of wood or bones

that appear in the story are available to touch and pass around.)

- *What makes a good story teller?* (Someone who can make many facial expressions, use different inflections to the volume and tone of voice, and show physical gestures that dramatize what is said.)
- *When and where are stories told?* (At night around the cooking fire when the moon is out, and sometimes at grandfather's house. Also, grandmothers will tell stories to children most any time that is appropriate.)
- *Why are stories told?* (For entertainment, to remember important things about our tribe, and to instruct the children on how to behave.)
- *How long is each traditional story?* (That all depends on the situation. Sometimes they are very short; other times quite long depending on the attention being given by the listeners.)
- *What are the differences in telling a true story and a fable?* (True stories contain facts and names of real people and places. We decided to never start a story with "once upon a time" and to always end the oral version of each Bible story with these words: "A true story from the Bible.")

Andrea wrote, "These stories are similar to what Grandma [Leilah E. Runyon, to whom this book is dedicated] did with her Sunday school flannel graph stories. The main points of the Bible story must be there, but the oral stories don't have to have all the details of a written Bible translation. However, any details included must be accurate and used based on the interests of the audience."

Andrea said a good translator for a written translation does *not* necessarily make a good translator for an oral Bible story. This was encouraging, since my "team" consisted of 15 Bible school students who had never done this before. However, it worked because they were telling stories for their own people, to be shared in traditional ways and comfortable settings.

"There are certain kinds of understanding that we have no access to except by means of story" writes Marilyn Chandler McEntyre (*Caring for Words in a Culture of Lies,* Grand Rapids: Eerdmans, 2009): "Stories invite us to reflect on . . . basic questions. How do things happen? How are they related? What have they to do with us?" (113). "They offer the kind of knowing that comes in glimpses, moments, flashes of memory, associations" (114).

In Malawi, our purpose for writing the stories was first to imprint them on the minds of the story tellers. Students then practiced telling their stories without looking at their notes. At the end of the telling, they were encouraged to ask questions of their listeners. The discussion questions below derive from those recommended by Christine Dillon (*Telling the Gospel Through Story,* 201-202):

Set 1

1. What do you like best about this story? Why?
2. What do you struggle with or not understand?
3. What do you learn about people?
4. What do you learn about God?
5. What needs to change in your life after hearing this story?

Set 2

1. What truths do you see in this story?
2. Which truth matters most to you?
3. How could this truth change your life?
4. Who else needs to hear this story?

Of course, specific questions can also be developed to fit with each individual story.

The length of the *Tribal Bible* stories was dictated by the amount that could be written by hand on one sheet of notebook paper in a place where paper is scarce (but occasionally, for the longer stories, students requested a second sheet of paper).

May this project be replicated many times over until the day comes when the word of God has been put into the minds and written on the hearts of everyone in all tribes so that all will know God from the most important chiefs to the least of the women and children (Jer. 31:33-34).

—Daniel V. Runyon, Editor

Homework

Fred Bamus — world mission — Chichewa and English

YESU akwera Kunka Kumwamba ACTS 1:1-11
Jesus ascend into heaven

Buku la Machitidwe lidanena zonse zomwe Yesu adayamba Kuzichita ndi kuzipunmutsa kufikira tsiku lomwe adakwera Kumwamba. The book of Acts mention all things Jesus started to do and teach up to the day he was taken into heaven. Atamaliza zonse mwa mzimu woyera adadziwonetsa atumwi omwe adamuona Yesu wamoyo, masiku makumi anayi adzaonekera kwa masiku makumi anayi pundaniza' za ufumu wakumwamba. After he finished teaching them in Holy Spirit and being shown himself to his disciples alive for forty days teaching them the good news of kingdom of God. Anawa lamulira asachoke ku yerusalemu koma adikire lonjezano la atate kuti abatizidwe ndi mzimu oyera. He ordered them not to move from Jerusalem but wait the promise of God that they will recieve the Holy Spirit. Anammusa yesu ngati ntchentcha adzatuwerera ufumu kwa ayisilayeri ndipo adawauza akhu kuti sikuli kwa iwo kudziwa nthawi ndi nyengo zomwe Mulungu adaziika. They asked Jesus if he would return the kingdom of Jews on that time but Jesus told them that it was not their responsibility to know the time and condition which God set for his own plan. Koma kuti adzalandira mphamvu Mzimu oyera atadza pa iwo ndipo adzakhala mboni zake mu Yerusalemu, Mwdeya ndi kusa mabga komanso kumalekezero adziko lapansi. But that they would recieve the power when Holy Spirit come upon them and that they would be his witnesses to the Jerusalem, all Judea and Samaria and to the very end of the world. Ndipo mmene adanena izi ati chiponyere iwo, Yesu adatengedwa kupita kumwamba ndipo

DANNY MUNKONDIA

GOD'S WRATH EXPLAINED - ROMANS 1:18-32

* Ubukalale bwa chala bwamamvikna ukufuma kumwanya kubabomba mbibi bosi kwambula kwitikizya ububibi nuku zyaghama ukuti uchala akwivwisya lubilo sona nukuti vingoba bwibubu.
- God's fierce anger is being made known from heaven against all their godliness and wickedness from men who withhold from the truth by their wickedness, so that they must know, God is easily understood to them

* and He has made to be so.
* Akabala ka chala, umvwismaka bhosi nububeli bukubonska namo akapelela.
- God's invisible character, his eternal power and divine nature have been and understood from what have been made.

* Nanga buli bamumenye uchala loli batakumukwiezya nukumupata.
- Although they never glorified God or give thanks to him, they knew him.

* Inninangano zyabo zili kuvifwami, nimyoyo yabo yili muchisi.
- Their minds became idle and foolish hearts were darkness.

* Bakuboneka ngati ba mahala loli havgha.
- They seems to be intelligent but they were not.

* Ubukulu bwa chala bakusendite ngati bwa munthu cia ninyamana pamo bara viyuni.
- The glory of immortal God's image they made like mortal man, birds and animals.

* Uchala akabapa ubulamuliro pakabibi kosi akapo moyo wabo mukunyenyezya umubili wabo.
- God gave them over in sinful desire of their hearts to sexual impurity for degrading of their bodies.

* Bakusinthania ubwamaloli bwa tata uchala nubumuasi, bakwiputa kuvipailwa mwmalo mwakwiputa umupeli.
- They exchange the truth of God with lie, they worship this creation instead of creator.

* Uchala akabapela umubili wabo mwize lou bakusinthana

HAWA PHIRI

WORLD MISSION

THE STORY OF THE TRANSFORMED ONES
ROMANS 11:33 - 12:2   TONGA AND ENGLISH LANGUAGE

Ha threw wake wa kuchuta ndi zeni zake nal tugwa a. ndi lulekci kupenzika kwake wamsulu kilonde kyeseka Paulo ndumbilwa. Paul was encourage the church Oh the powerful of God and his knowledge and his wisdom and who is knowing his judgment.
Ninga

Ninga kumb ndugani wangazwa ntima waka chud a panankaga mpungi wader ndugani.
And who knows his heart or the his counselor or God.

Ninga ndugani mwakumae vowangwenba kumpatsa chuch ndips ijo wazamuwereserapa.
Who was started to gave him things that God is also give n them.
Ndic

Ndichu chirulewu chake chechosi cho thotulya kwaka chipita chinatsa ku mweneka chitefa ndip kwa yo kuwenge wernetara wa muyaya amen
That's why everything who some from him is through him and is also happened through him and to Him, be received praised forever and forever Amen.

Nchikululawa chake ndetikupomphani inwe mwa abadal le ndingu mwa lisungu lakuchuta kuti muperke mali waro ngiri kwwa sembi ya moyo yakunpatuka yakukondo wetsa chuto.
That's why my brothers in Jesus Christ I ask you to give your bodies as living sercerice to God and pleasing God with pure heart and spiritual act.

A story in the Tonga language with English translation based on Romans 11:33-12:2.

Acknowledgments

Partial funding for this, my fifth trip to Malawi, came from the Spring Arbor University International Initiatives Committee, and from friends, relatives, and prayer partners at the University and at Spring Arbor Free Methodist Church. My wife, Renee, and son Caleb, were co-teachers and partners in this adventure.

Special thanks to my 15 world missions students in Malawi who wrote the stories and whose names also appear throughout the book with their entries: Fred. K. Bamus, McPherson Janaia Banda, Nelson Banda, Blessings Chagomerana, MacDonald Chikankheni, Ronald Chinkonde, George Chikoya, Lemiter Kachinjika, George Lupande, Danny Steven Munkondia, Chifundo Patrick, Hawa Phiri, Paul Alufasi Phiri, Winiko Wanyetha, Billiat William.

Thanks to Kwade Joslin for designing this book cover, and thanks to the editors who fixed my many mistakes: G. Harry Bonney, Alexandra Harper, and Renée Runyon.

—*Daniel V. Runyon*, Editor

Dedication

In memory of Leilah E. Runyon (1915-1997).
Mom loved to tell the story of Jesus and his love.

Cemetery marker photo by Mary Runyon Metzger

www.ingramcontent.com/pod-product-compliance
Lightning Source LLC
Chambersburg PA
CBHW031319160426
43196CB00007B/581